100 20TH-CENTURY SPORTS & LEISURE BUILDINGS

100 20TH-CENTURY SPORTS & LEISURE BUILDINGS

The Twentieth Century Society

Edited by Susannah Charlton & Alistair Fair
New photography by John East

BATSFORD

BATSFORD

Editor **Rebecca Armstrong**
Art Director **Eoghan O'Brien**
Junior Designer **Sanya Jain**
Layout design by **Kei Ishimaru**
Head of Production **Morna McPherson**
Production Controller **Pete Rouse**
Publishing Manager **Nicola Newman**

First published in the United Kingdom
in 2025 by

Batsford
43 Great Ormond Street
London
WC1N 3HZ

An imprint of B. T. Batsford Holdings Limited

Copyright © B. T. Batsford Ltd 2025

Text copyright © C20 Society 2025

All rights reserved. No part of this publication may be copied, displayed, extracted, reproduced, utilized, stored in a retrieval system or transmitted in any form or by any means, electronic, mechanical or otherwise including but not limited to photocopying, recording, or scanning without the prior written permission of the publishers.

ISBN 9781849949408

A CIP catalogue record for this book is available from the British Library.

10 9 8 7 6 5 4 3 2 1

Reproduction by Rival Colour Ltd, UK
Printed and bound by Toppan Leefung Printing International Ltd, China

This book can be ordered direct from the publisher at www.batsfordbooks.com, or try your local bookshop.

PREVIOUS PAGE Center Parcs, Nottinghamshire (1987).

CONTENTS

6	Introduction **Alistair Fair**
12	1914–1929
40	1930–1939
56	Lidos **Alan Powers**
86	1940–1969
100	Sports Stadiums **Simon Inglis**
146	1970–1989
164	The Leisure Centre Boom **Otto Saumarez Smith**
200	1990–1999
218	2000–present
246	Further Reading
247	Acknowledgements
248	Picture Credits
249	Index

INTRODUCTION

This book is about buildings for sports and leisure constructed in England, Scotland and Wales since 1914. On the one hand, the selection presented here tells a story of architectural diversity and innovation. It reveals something of the ebb and flow of traditionalism and modernity in twentieth-century architecture, showing how designers and their clients sought to create places which were not only functional, but which also conveyed particular ideas about the sports they housed. At the same time, the significance of these buildings also reflects their role in people's lives. Even for those who are not keen sporting participants themselves, sports and leisure buildings often conjure up strong memories, from childhood birthday parties in swimming pools to the excitement and camaraderie of watching a team competing out on the pitch.

Although the construction of purpose-built spaces for sports and leisure dates back centuries, taking in such examples as the baths of the ancient Roman Empire or the 'real tennis' courts of the sixteenth century, the foundations of a new architecture of sport and leisure – and, indeed, modern sports and leisure – were laid during the nineteenth century. This period saw the rise of organized sport. The shiftwork which underpinned industrialization and later the emergence of office-based jobs created clearly defined periods of 'non-working time', while urbanization not only concentrated the population but also led to demands for buildings and spaces in which a degree of respite from wider urban conditions might be offered. In these circumstances, expanding Victorian towns and cities built swimming baths as symbols of municipal pride and ambition. Major urban employers constructed sports and social clubs for their workers. New suburbs featured golf courses, whose open green areas contributed to the arcadian quality of their surroundings. Sports stadia drew thousands on a regular basis, contributing to the formation of new communities and identities.

While private and commercial interests have always had a role to play in creating and operating places dedicated to sport and leisure, the selection of buildings in this book illustrates the rise of the state during the twentieth century, at both the local and national levels. Until the 1950s, provision, especially for swimming, was very much the preserve of local authorities, but subsequently leisure also assumed greater significance at a national policy level. Predictions of ever-increasing amounts of free time – created by automation, efficiency and computers, as well as by reductions in the working week and increased paid holiday entitlement – meant that provision for 'leisure' was a major concern by the 1960s. The Sports Council was formed in 1965 to oversee spending in ways that echoed those of the Arts Council, founded 20 years before, while an increasingly diverse range of facilities was offered to the

OPPOSITE Bletchley Leisure Centre (1973), with steel pyramid above the swimming pool. Despite C20 objections, the centre was demolished in 2009.

ABOVE University of Liverpool Sports Centre. Denys Lasdun and Partners (1963–6).

public. In this respect, the post-war story, in particular, is one of evolution, moving from an emphasis on health, fitness and self-improvement to one in which new agendas such as 'leisure' and fun were to the fore. New fashions were embraced, from squash in the 1960s to roller-skating in the 1970s and skateboarding in the 1980s. New building types were invented, including multi-functional leisure centres (from the 1960s) and skateparks (from the late 1970s).

Sports and leisure architecture also illustrates the history of modernism, as well as its diversity. During the 1930s, 'Art Deco' styling imbued lidos with a fashionable touch of glamour. Modern architecture's lack of ornament and frequently large windows evoked ideas of cleanliness and health, while concrete and steel construction drove innovation in stadium design and created clear-span spaces of sometimes dramatic character in the case of the Empire Pool at Wembley (1934) or Aberdeen's Bon Accord Baths (1940). Yet in other cases, the connotations provided by traditional styles were preferred, creating an image felt to be appropriate in such locations as golf courses and tennis clubs.

The long period of post-war austerity meant that the construction of 'non-essential' buildings did not resume until the end of the 1950s. By then, modernism dominated architectural practice generally in Britain, with the picturesque, often decorative style of the Festival of Britain (1951) being increasingly joined by the boldly massed forms, directly expressed materials and structural gymnastics that were characteristic of Brutalism. As a result, the new generation of post-war leisure buildings contrasted dramatically in terms of their appearance with their Victorian, Edwardian and inter-war predecessors.

There was a particular boom in swimming pool construction from c.1960 to 1966. Ambitious provision reflected a sense that Britain had a shortage of swimming pools; meanwhile, the 1944 Education Act (in England and Wales) required that all children learn to swim. There were major developments for swimming in the new towns, while established local authorities sought to replace older Victorian baths, now seen as architecturally and functionally outdated (not least as they frequently housed separate pools for men and women, segregated also according to class). The pool in which I myself learned to swim, Tudor Grange in Solihull, was part of this boom, opening in 1964; it was demolished and rebuilt c. 2008. In parallel with these developments, the Wolfenden Report of 1960 highlighted a shortage of facilities for indoor sports other than swimming, and so prompted the construction of multi-functional centres; the National Recreation Centre at Crystal Palace was an early example (designed, in fact, from 1953), as was provision at Harlow (1959) and Billingham (1967). The new and expanding universities of this period also frequently built for sports and leisure, exploiting a funding loophole which allowed them to secure public funding provided they accommodate examinations at least twice a year, with centres at Hull, Keele, Liverpool, Sussex, Birmingham and St Andrews being among the best-equipped in Europe at the time of their construction.

These buildings' modern image embedded them in the wider programme of construction which saw Britain's towns and cities transformed during this period, with the dramatic forms of major structures like Cardiff's Wales Empire Pool (1958), Coventry's Central Baths (1966) or the Dollan Baths in East Kilbride (1968) embodying in new ways the ideas of civic pride that had shaped their Victorian forebears. As local government reorganization loomed in the late 1960s and early 1970s, some authorities, such as Billingham on Teesside, blew their capital reserves on the construction of facilities rather than hand the money to their successors.

Yet the modernism of these buildings was more than a matter of appearance. They often depended on ever more complex systems of heating, ventilation and lighting, while the structural possibilities offered by reinforced concrete, steel and laminated timber made possible the construction of ever-larger, column-free spaces. Not only were newly popular sports such as squash accommodated, but established building types were rethought. For example, the serried poolside cubicles of older swimming baths were replaced by new layouts in which changing took place below vast banks of spectator seating. Facilities were made for learners and diving enthusiasts, and large windows allowed views out and in. Standardized dimensions were set down for pools, in terms of length (33.5 metres or 110 feet to accommodate county championships) and depth (a minimum of 0.9 metres or 3 feet, to allow water polo).

New design approaches also transformed the image of commercial leisure and organized sport. The daring concrete forms of Peter Womersley's Gala Fairydean stadium (1964) demonstrate well the ways in which the image and experience of spectating could be rethought. That said, many stadia remained relatively rudimentary for much of the twentieth century. Cantilevered stadium seating began to appear in the 1930s, and developed from the end of the 1950s, but it was only after the Hillsborough tragedy of 1989 that a new focus on safety and the requirement that large stadia be all-seated prompted a more considered approach to design and layout generally.

By the 1980s, what had previously seemed like the certainties of modernism were increasingly being questioned. Some sought to re-invent modernism through an appeal to engineering and technology, prompting the High Tech steel and fabric membranes of Lord's Cricket Ground (1987). Others, however, sought to appeal to architecture's past, often in playful and witty ways which made the resulting postmodernism the ideal style for a new generation of leisure centres. The rise of this type of building during the 1970s, 80s and 90s suggested a new role for the state as the enabler of fun. Subsequently, the advent of National Lottery funding after 1994 spurred the creation of a new generation of often generously specified buildings, some intended for professional as well as community users, while the 2012 London Olympics not only led to the construction of bespoke buildings by leading designers but also promised to create a new landscape of places for sport and participation.

Yet more than a decade of falling levels of public spending since then has resulted in the loss of sports and leisure facilities. Despite the clear health benefits of participating or even just spectating, some places remain at risk, with their opening hours reduced and maintenance cut back; they are sometimes dependent on volunteers to survive. C20's 'Leisure Centres Campaign' was launched in 2022 following successful moves to save the Oasis Leisure Centre in Swindon, and so far has resulted in the protection of several centres through statutory listing. But it is not only leisure centres or other local authority facilities which face challenges. The rise of technology, the popularity of home-based leisure, a failure to attract young members plus the impacts of the Covid-19 pandemic, have all hastened the closure of some privately run facilities such as tennis and bowls clubs, their valuable urban sites often being earmarked for housing. In some cases, people have mobilized to take over assets for community use – as in, for example, the case of a former bowls club in Pollokshields, Glasgow, which now accommodates a range of activities. And the local support given to C20's campaigns shows just how important sports and leisure buildings can be for those who live near them and use them. The creation of a new generation of private gyms and sports complexes shows that there is a demand for well-specified facilities, though architecturally these centres are rarely of note.

In these circumstances, then, the following compendium aims to shed light on the startling variety of structures built since 1914 for sports and leisure, ranging the length and breadth of England, Scotland and Wales. Our selection brings together the well known and the obscure, by designers ranging from the internationally famous to those who developed a specialism in a particular type of structure. It is a selection which includes avant-garde radicalism as well as quiet traditionalism. We hope that it will, at the very least, encourage you to find out more about these buildings and to support C20's work by joining the society or coming to events. And maybe some readers will even feel inclined to take up a new sport!

Alistair Fair

1914 – 1929

Beaconsfield Golf Clubhouse

Location: Beaconsfield, Buckinghamshire
Designed by: Stanley Hinge Hamp of Collcutt & Hamp
Opened: 1914
Listed: Grade II

One of the last significant golf course expansions before the First World War, Beaconsfield Golf Club offers a charming fantasy of Merrie England. Mixing a richly decorated medieval interior with a relaxed Tudorbethan cottage exterior, it adjoins an 18-hole course designed by leading golf course architect Henry Shapland Colt.

The brick and clay-tiled clubhouse is replete with carefully resolved and picturesque details, including two large decorative chimney stacks, which dominate the composition. While some of these details have been lost over the years, most notably the open brickwork parapet on the west façade, and the cross-hatched brickwork balustrade above the loggia, many others remain. These include circular rubbed brick columns in antis along the west elevation and the deeply recessed circular windows that flank each end of the principal elevation. The largely intact, medieval-style interior has timber panelling, oversized oak framing, plaster friezes and an abundance of carved figures.

Andrew Murray

York Racecourse Clock Tower and Indicator Boards

Location: York, North Yorkshire
Designed by: Walter Brierley of Brierley & Rutherford
Opened: 1922
Listed: Grade II

The racecourse clocktower sits prominently on a grass-covered viewing bank, within the ring of the racetrack and opposite the main stands. Accommodation for the Tote and toilets is hidden below and accessible from behind. Brierley maintained the elegant Neo-Georgian style used in his other racecourse buildings, here taking inspiration from buildings such as the garden house at Westbury Court, Gloucestershire, and eighteenth-century market halls.

It is square on plan and steel framed with a reconstituted stone Doric-columned loggia. The double-height indicator-board room is timber clad and on three sides has full height changeable boards, which list the races and runners. It has a hipped slated roof with a cupola clock. The loggia is two-storeyed on the west elevation and the upper room has shuttered windows. Purcell Architects led an extensive restoration in 2018 and it remains a much-loved landmark in the western enclosure, now renamed the Clocktower Enclosure.

Simon Green

All England Lawn Tennis and Croquet Club

Location: Church Road, Wimbledon, London
Designed by: Charles Stanley Peach
Opened: 1922

Despite hosting the oldest Grand Slam tennis championship, being a venue for the 2012 Olympic Games, and with parts of its Centre Court dating to the club's move to the present site in 1922, no single element of Wimbledon's tennis stadia, hospitality and ancillary buildings is listed as architecturally significant.

Today's ambience results from consecutive long-term masterplans: from the 1990s in the hands of BDP; from 2011 by Grimshaw. A major expansion into adjacent parkland is now planned by Allies and Morrison.

The pervasive colours of the club have been dark green and purple since 1909, the combination finally trademarked only in 2016. The famous 'Henman Hill' big-screen venue dates from the 1990s re-ordering. Ingenious engineering is perhaps the greatest wonder after the players: the stately closing of the mighty concertina-style translucent roofs on Centre and No. 1 courts. The club's large new indoor clay-court tennis centre by Hopkins is first-rate.

Hugh Pearman

Longniddry Golf Clubhouse

Location: Links Road, Longniddry, East Lothian
Designed by: James Davidson Cairns
Opened: 1922
Listed: Category B

When Longniddry was expanded after the First World War, landowner and keen golfer, the 11th Earl of Wemyss, appointed Henry Shapland Colt to design an 18-hole course on his Gosford Estate, with spectacular views across to Edinburgh and the Fife coast. The Arts and Crafts clubhouse, with club master's house to the rear, was erected in stages, with seven years separating the two-storey main entrance block and lower, flat-roofed, courtyard-style service wing to the west. Linking them is a double-height square outlook tower, with corner window, ogee roof and weather vane. On the west façade are ball finials and an armorial panel salvaged from eighteenth-century Amisfield House, which was demolished in 1928–9.

The walls are of honey-coloured rubble stone, and the roofs hipped and slated. The entrance façade is gabled with a keystoned oculus and window bay, and an additional flat-roofed bay to the west once functioned as the starter's box. The cosy interior has an inglenook fireplace in the lounge and panelled entrance hall.

Fiona Sinclair

Cricket Pavilion, Upper Field, Uppingham School

Location: Uppingham, Rutland
Designed by: Michael Tapper
Opened: 1923
Listed: Grade II

Uppingham's first cricket pavilion, an iron shed, was succeeded in 1864 by a brick pavilion with an elegant veranda. On the ground's west side, it encroached on the playing area and eventually became outdated and too small.

A better site, in the north-west corner, was found for this new pavilion. It was designed by Old Uppinghamian (and good sportsman) Michael John Tapper, son of ecclesiastical architect Walter John Tapper; they were in partnership from 1920. The stone-built pavilion offered an Arts and Crafts version of classic pavilion design. Picturesque thatching was topped by a circular turret housing the cricket bell; wooden panelling inside the long room carried honours boards; while the central gable's clock hung above the scoring box and balcony. Due to structural problems, the balcony was removed in 2001, but reinstated during a thorough 2023–4 renovation by SDC, which also enhanced the interior.

Lynn Pearson

Tennis Clubhouse

Location: Ashworth Lane, Bolton, Lancashire
Opened: 1923
Listed: Grade II

This mock-timber tennis clubhouse by an unknown designer was built as an amenity for mill workers living in the model village of Bank Top. The village was established in the nineteenth century to serve the New Eagley Mills, owned by the Quaker Ashworth family. Although the mills had stopped spinning in 1880, they operated as weaving mills until 1940. The single-storey building has three bays with a pedimented gable above the central entrance, a decorative entablature on wrought-iron brackets and a cupola with a weather vane on the roof. Its Neo-Tudor style was a popular choice for suburban developments in the 1920s. The clubhouse was extended in 1935.

The tennis courts are the only major area of open space in the village, and form part of the Bank Top Conservation Area. The clubhouse that once served beer now houses the Bank Top Brewery, which brews 22,000 pints a week for local pubs.

Susannah Charlton

Rowheath Pavilion

Location: Bournville, Birmingham, West Midlands
Designed by: John Ramsay Armstrong
Opened: 1924
Listed: Grade II

This sports pavilion was built on the playing fields of the Cadbury's Chocolate Factory in Bournville, serving the games played by the expanded workforce – soccer, cricket, hockey, rugby, tennis, croquet, bowling, athletics – and also acting as a venue for a range of social activities. Its main two-storey rendered brick elevation faces the grounds, with a long, arcaded ground floor between staircase turrets, a veranda above with tiled balustrade, large first floor windows, a tiled roof with central clock turret, and lower two-storey wings, the ensemble carrying more than a little hint of large cricket pavilions in India. It is set on a terrace looking down onto the boating lake.

The roadside elevation was extended several times and the grounds developed for housing. Despite this the building's form and plan remain largely intact, and it was listed in 2017. It is now occupied by the Trinity Christian Centre Trust.

Katriona Byrne

Victoria Bowling Club

Location: Norwich, Norfolk
Designed by: Albert Havers
Opened: 1926

The Victoria Bowling Club was founded in 1870. It expanded during the interwar period, as the suburbs developed. In 1925, John Youngs, local builder and newly elected Vice-President, donated a small thatched-roof shelter aside the green. A grander, symmetrically fronted, half-timbered and thatched pavilion followed in 1926, designed by Havers, Secretary and local architect, and built by Youngs. Both speak to Stockbroker's Tudor, but the pavilion with its veranda is also an imperial typology.

Havers' most notable building, also in Norwich, is the chunkily baroque former Masonic Hall of 1907 (Grade II Listed). The pavilion's construction coincided with Havers' admission as a Fellow of the RIBA, and he died just four years later. In 1972 a firework landed on the thatched roof of the main pavilion, setting it alight. It was re-roofed with tile and the adjoining locker room built. The smaller shelter has been re-thatched in recent years.

Matthew Lloyd Roberts

Stanley Park

Location: Blackpool, Lancashire
Designed by: Thomas Mawson & Sons
Opened: 1926
Listed: Grade II*

Stanley Park was built in the aftermath of the First World War and heralded a new kind of park, inspired by fresh ideas about youth, health and exercise. Having been on the periphery of Victorian parks dominated by promenades, flower beds, seats and statuary, sports and games were now centre stage. With legislation and the rise of unions ensuring for the first time a week's paid holiday to thousands of workers, the Blackpool Corporation was keen to attract the thousands for whom Blackpool became the seaside resort of choice.

The park took four years to construct and was opened in 1926. It incorporated a pre-existing cricket square, athletics track and nine-hole golf course, together with acres of new bowling greens and football pitches. The sports provision was complemented by formal gardens, and a 22-acre (9-hectare) lake, and later an Art Deco restaurant, all restored in the early 2000s with a large National Heritage Lottery grant.

David Lambert

30

Ynysangharad Lido (National Lido of Wales)

Location: Pontypridd, Rhondda Cynon Taf
Designed by: William Lowe, Surveyor, Pontypridd District Council
Opened: 1927
Listed: Grade II

There was an interwar boom in providing open-air swimming baths across South Wales. Unemployment schemes, a Labour government, and charitable trusts funded improved sport and leisure opportunities. With £1,500 from the Miners' Welfare Fund, William Lowe fought for a facility the town could 'look on with pride'. Despite being scaled down, his design of a double-ended pool, with central semi-circular diving area, accommodated 1,000 swimmers and serviced high-profile aquatic events from swimming races to water polo. The low, white-rendered, Arts and Crafts pavilion and 50 changing cubicles roofed in red pantiles referenced Roman villas and the bathhouse at Caerleon. This was enhanced by using fountains to pump fresh water into the centre of the pool, maintaining the aesthetics of a practical pumping system.

The lido underwent a £6.3 million restoration between 1991 and 2015. The only surviving listed lido in Wales, it has provided inspiration for a new generation of open-air swimmers.

Susan Fielding

Northumberland Baths

Location: Newcastle upon Tyne, Northumberland
Designed by: Nicholas & Dixon-Spain
Opened: 1928
Listed: Grade II

After a competition in 1924 judged by swimming pool specialist Alfred Cross, the design for the baths and City Hall concert venue was a building in the Neo-Georgian style typical of interwar civic architecture. Its brown brick façade, with ashlar dressings and a Doric portico, hides a steel frame.

Inside are two pool halls – the larger men's one has a cantilevered viewing gallery and coffered ceiling, the simpler 25-metre women's pool no gallery. Turkish baths in the basement have Doric pilasters, mahogany-panelled changing rooms and individual resting beds, a steam room with marble slabs and a domed ceiling. In winter the pools were floored over for other uses, which included being used as a cinema. After they closed in 2013, user group Friends of City Baths campaigned for their re-opening, supporting Fusion Lifestyle's recent refurbishment. The women's pool and Turkish baths have been restored and a gym and two-level exercise studios inserted within the men's pool.

Susannah Charlton

Highfields Park

Location: Nottingham, East Midlands
Designed by: Percy Morley Horder
Opened: 1923
Listed: Grade II

Highfields Park was given to Nottingham by Methodist Sir Jesse Boot, of Boots the Chemist, after shareholders objected to his intention of building a model factory and village. Instead, he created a public park upon the flood plain and a university campus on the hills to the north. The centrepiece is the Trent Building (1922–8) and boating lake, combining neo-classical architecture, Beaux-arts planning and picturesque landscaping, by Boots' own architect. An axial plan aligns with the University Boulevard; campanile, terracing, lake, pathway, gateway and a bronze bust of Lord Trent. Either side lie the bowling and croquet pavilions; neo-classical with Moderne canopies facing the lawns. The original lakeside pavilion and lido have been replaced by Julian Marsh's contextual modernist Lakeside Arts Centre (2003) and the modest postmodern Djanogly Gallery (1996). Morley Horder's boating stage is still in use. Highfields Park has a little bit of everything for everyone. How very Methodist.

Chris Matthews

Ramsgate Croquet and Bowling Pavilions

Location: Royal Esplanade, Ramsgate, Kent
Designed by: Franklin & Deacon
Opened: 1929
Listed: Grade II

In the 1920s, the clifftop land between Ramsgate's west cliff and Pegwell Bay was developed to provide a new approach road, homes and resort facilities. A 30-acre (12-hectare) strip of seafront was laid out with two 18-hole putting greens, a bowling green, tennis courts, a miniature golf course and a central bandstand (which was later replaced by a boating pool). The area was formally opened by Ramsgate's Mayor in July 1929. Shelters, low walls and embanked hedges provide a degree of protection from the wind, while in 1928 Basil C. Deacon (not J. J. Burnet, as is sometimes supposed) of Luton-based firm Franklin & Deacon, designed bowls and tennis pavilions in the Italian Renaissance style. Ramsgate Croquet Club moved to this location in 1987 and levelled the present lawns using lasers. The bowling green next door is the home of the Ramsgate Bowling Club and is open from April to September.

Geraint Franklin

Porchester Centre

Location: Porchester Road, Paddington, London
Designed by: Herbert Shepherd, Borough Architect
Opened: 1925
Listed: Grade II*

The Metropolitan Borough of Paddington built the Porchester Centre in phases between 1923 and 1929. As well as its celebrated Turkish baths, there are two swimming pools, assembly halls and a public library. The steel-framed building has a sober exterior made of Portland stone and red, purple and stock brick. The main pool is lined with moulded faience. The windows set in the barrel-vaulted ceiling make for quite gloomy swimming.

The Turkish bath is a world apart. Its entrance features an original inlaid marble floor. Double doors lead to the lounge area and the staircase to a plunge pool and hot rooms of increasing heat. There is also a shampooing room featuring original marble slab tables. One of the many fine qualities of this building is the way in which the world of municipal cleanliness and health is complemented by the mysteries of the steam, the heat and the very low lighting.

Paul Lincoln

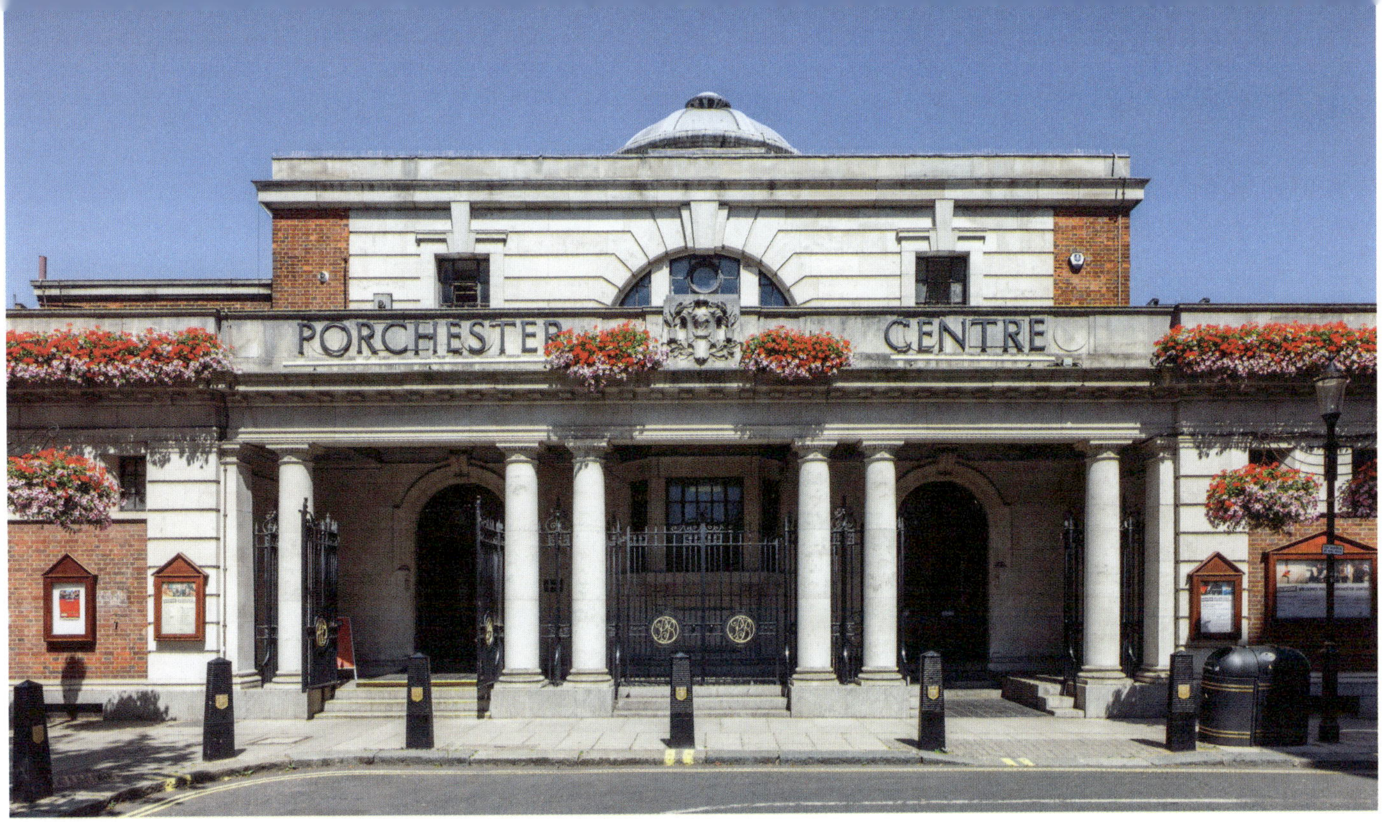
PORCHESTER CENTRE

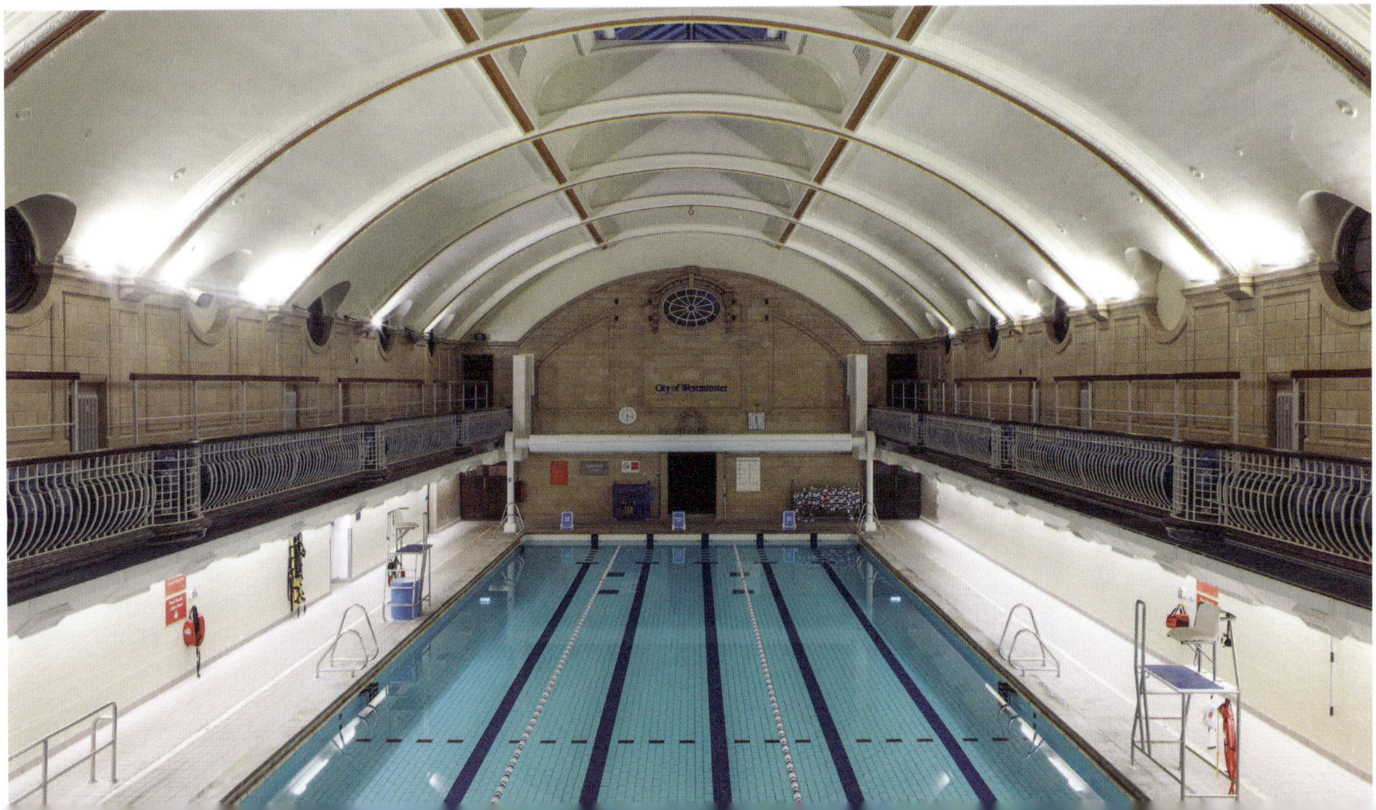
City of Westminster

Ibrox Stadium South Stand (formerly Ibrox Park)

Location: Edmiston Drive, Glasgow
Designed by: Archibald Leitch & Partners
Opened: 1929
Listed: Category B

Perhaps reflecting the symbiotic relationship between industry and mass leisure, the mighty red brick and stone south façade of Rangers' stadium in industrialized Clydeside resembles a factory. It officially held up to 75,000 spectators following expanded terracing in 1902, designed by Archibald Leitch. Tragically, only months after completion, part of this collapsed, killing 25 people. Leitch, a Rangers supporter, was deeply affected and became very conscious of crowd safety.

The South Stand was completed in 1929, also by Leitch and architecturally the finest of his many football terraces. The central portico, with arched and pedimented windows, is flanked by wings, each of ten bays with stair towers at each end. Inside were two tiers, the lower for standees and the upper a balcony seating 10,000. In the early 1990s, a third tier of seating was added, resulting in the new roof and hi-tech space-frame girders, which protrude above the existing frontage.

Bruce Peter

1930–1939

Barrie (Cricket) Pavilion

Location: Hill of Kirriemuir, Angus
Designed by: Frank Drummond Thomson
Opened: 1930
Listed: Category B

No longer used for cricket matches, Kirriemuir's sandstone and harled park pavilion, gifted to the 'Wee Red Toon' by J. M. Barrie, is now home to a small museum, tearoom and purpose-built camera obscura, one of only three in Scotland. Won in competition by Frank Thomson, the building originally had changing rooms and toilets on either side of a wood-lined reception room, with the camera obscura in an octagonal attic space above the main entrance, giving live images of the Angus Glens and Grampian foothills. Barrie, author of *Peter Pan* and lifelong cricket enthusiast, captained a team including fellow writers Arthur Conan Doyle and A. A. Milne, and is buried in the nearby cemetery, whose iron gate once served as fixed wickets for the local team.

Raised on a broad viewing terrace, this modest pavilion is now run by the volunteers of the Kirriemuir Regeneration Group. Memorabilia on display includes score cards, commemorative cricket bats, books and paintings.

Fiona Sinclair

Summers Lane Sports Ground (grandstand)

Location: Finchley, London
Designed by: Percival T. Harrison
Opened: 1930
Listed: Grade II

This grandstand was built in 1930 for Finchley Urban District Council, most likely to the designs of the engineer Percival T. Harrison, with Owen Williams (engineer for the original Wembley Stadium) retained as checking engineer for the project. The grandstand was part of a large proposed municipal complex including an open-air lido (since demolished) and a town hall that was never built. The grandstand represents a first in the UK for possessing a cantilevered roof made of reinforced concrete, and it was opened in 1930 by Sir Frederick Wall, Secretary of the Football Association. It has been positively compared to the municipal stadium of Florence (1932) by Pier Luigi Nervi, which has a similar, larger concrete cantilevered canopy. Thanks to its back-to-back arrangement facing two pitches, the Summers Lane grandstand unusually serves both a football club and a rugby club – Wingate and Finchley FC and Finchley Rugby Club.

Joe Mathieson

The Royal Corinthian Yacht Club

Location: Burnham-on-Crouch, Essex
Designed by: Joseph Emberton
Opened: 1931
Listed: Grade II*

Under the aegis of a new Commodore, Philip Benson of Benson's Advertizing, the Royal Corinthian Yacht Club was modernizing. Women members were to be admitted, and a new clubhouse was needed. Benson commissioned Joseph Emberton (who had been the architectural director of the Advertizing Association's first exhibition in 1927), requesting a metal-framed structure of advanced design.

Emberton did not disappoint. Built on piles set into the foreshore, a steel frame supports a concrete platform, which allows three tiers of cantilevered balconies and the south-facing windows of the club's main rooms (including a mixed dining room and mixed lounge) to be almost entirely glazed. An external spiral iron staircase runs from first to top floor. From this machine for watching yachts, members had a commanding view of the Crouch on race days. Widely praised for the comfort of its accommodation, contemporaries were unanimous in appreciating that it was 'frankly modern in style.'

Elizabeth Darling

Tarlair Outdoor Pool

Location: Macduff, Aberdeenshire
Designed by: John Miller, Burgh Surveyor
Opened: 1931
Listed: Category A

Leaving the town of Macduff and descending into the picturesque bay, Tarlair is one of the few remaining outdoor pools in the UK from this period. Created 1929–35, its significance relates to its completeness and early use of concrete. The geometric reinforced concrete pavilion commands a spectacular view over John Miller's trio of pools. The largest is the boating lake (70 × 30 metres / 230 × 100 feet), with inset paddling pool. The lower seawater pool relied on a pump during the season (May to September), although the tide overtopped the seawall in the winter. Situated alongside are a changing block, and the pump house which also replenishes the upper pools with sea water. Sweeping concrete terraces enabled spectators to marvel at the courageous few leaping from the diving platforms.

    Since 2012 the Friends of Tarlair have maintained the crumbling site. In 2023, work started on the restoration of the pavilion, and the restoration of the pools will follow.

Chris Romer-Lee

Former Squash Court, Latymer School

Location: King St, Hammersmith, London
Designed by: J. E. M. Macgregor
Opened: 1932
Listed: Grade II

The squash court was built for novelist Naomi Mitchison and her husband Dick, in the back garden of their home, the eighteenth-century Rivercourt House. They were at the centre of a group of artists and writers that rivalled Bloomsbury. Macgregor was primarily known for historic conservation. In 1951 Latymer Upper School acquired the house and garden; the 1980s saw conversion into a music studio, with a mezzanine floor installed in 2016.

The building has three storeys fronted by a spiral staircase around a column topped by a seahorse weather vane. The side elevation has a gently curving crinkle-crankle wall, and an outdoor seating area with a bronze snail fountain. On the lintel are bas-reliefs depicting waves, vines, ears of wheat, a horse and a cockerel. The sculpture is by Gertrude Hermes, part of the Mitchisons' circle, known for her sculpture and mosaics at the Shakespeare Memorial Theatre in Stratford-upon-Avon.

Robert Drake

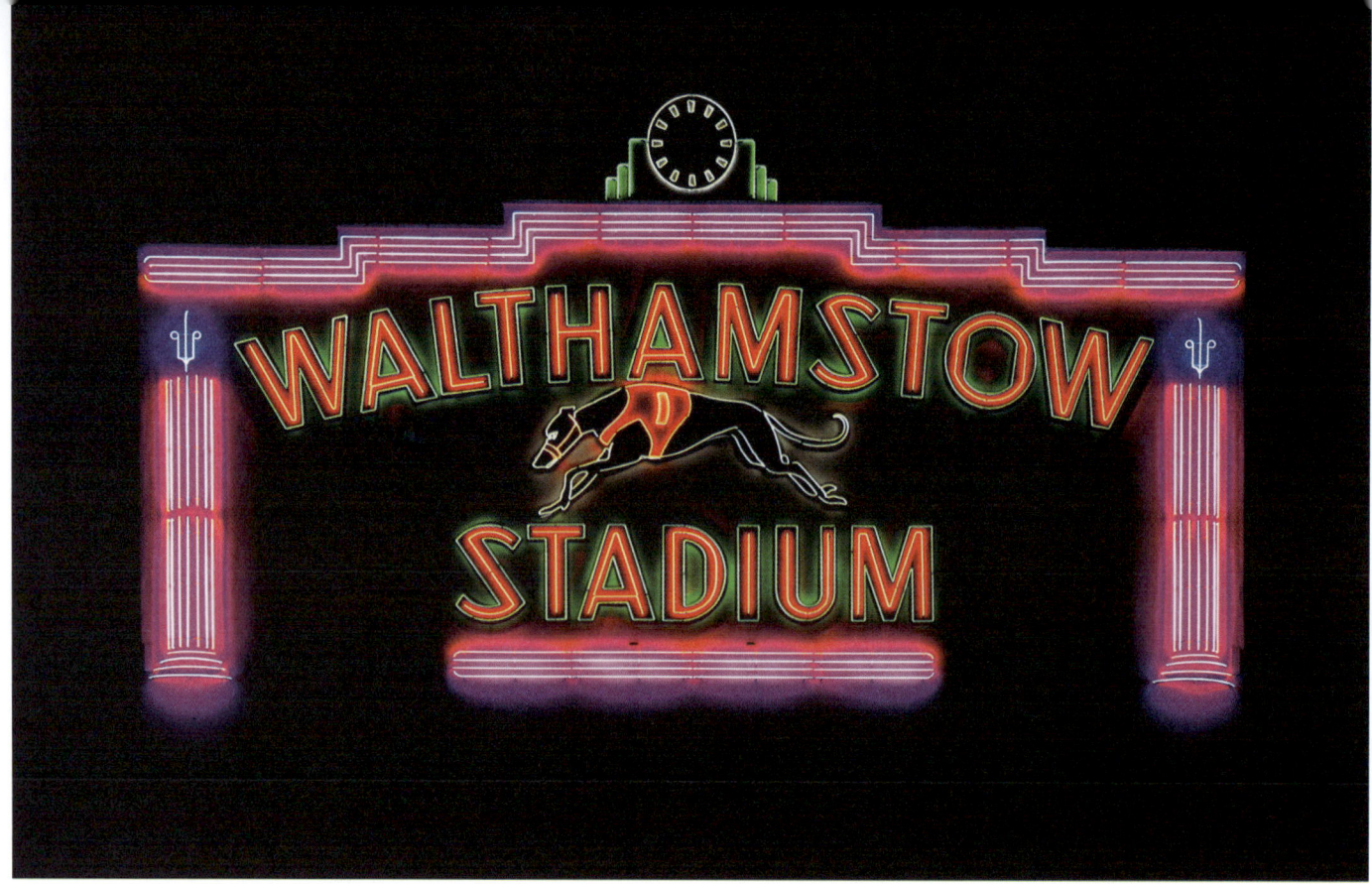

Walthamstow Stadium

Location: Chingford Road, Walthamstow, London
Opened: 1933
Listed: Grade II (entrance range and kennels)

In 2008, newspapers announced that the Walthamstow Stadium had 'run its course', as it closed for good. For about 75 years, it was a dynamic centre for greyhound racing, which arrived in England from the USA in the 1920s and became the new craze. Many of the racetracks set up in the early twentieth century have been lost, making Walthamstow a rare and important survivor.

William Chandler, leading bookie at White City and director of the Hackney Wick track, sold his shares in Hackney Wick to purchase the site at Walthamstow. The stadium has an iconic white Art Deco frontage, with 'Walthamstow Stadium' lit up by neon lights, installed in 1951 for Queen Elizabeth II's Coronation. Its entrance range, totaliser board and kennels survive. This East London landmark was the backdrop for everything from Winston Churchill's re-election campaign speech in 1945 to the launch of Britpop band Blur's album *Parklife* in 1994.

Coco Whittaker

Jockey Club

Location: Newmarket, Suffolk
Designed by: Albert Richardson
Opened: c.1933
Listed: Grade II

The Jockey Club commissioned a new building from Albert Richardson in the 1930s. Richardson, a master of contextualism, produced a design in the then fashionable Neo-Georgian style. The Jockey Club is an excellent example of his ability to create a sense of grandeur and timelessness, suitable for a building that acted as a social and administrative hub for horse racing enthusiasts.

The building's symmetrical layout, limestone arcade, enriched pilasters, cornice and frieze all reflect Richardson's deep appreciation for traditional architectural principles. His attention to detail and commitment to classical symmetry also blend well with the historic townscape of Newmarket. However, I must confess that, as a child spending my weekends in Newmarket, my attention was caught not by the Georgian allusions, but rather by the copper cupola and the statue of the racehorse Hyperion, winner of the 1933 Epsom Derby, in the front courtyard.

Clare Price

Smethwick Baths

Location: Smethwick, West Midlands
Designed by: Chester Button; Roland Fletcher, Borough Engineer
Opened: 1933
Listed: Grade II

Opening in 1933, civic aspiration was built into the fabric of Smethwick Baths: along with changing cubicles beside the pool, it originally had 24 slipper baths for public use and a café. The Moderne building has Art Deco interior detailing, with glazed tiling, terrazzo pilasters and floor, and decorated steel balustrades. Structural reinforced concrete parabolic arches frame the pool, an early echo of London's Royal Horticultural Halls (1928). Up until the 1970s, Smethwick Baths doubled as a venue: in winter months, the pool was covered with a sprung maple wood floor and used as a ballroom and concert hall; the Beatles performed here in November 1962. In July 2023, Smethwick Baths closed and was put up for sale by the Borough Council. In response, a campaign has since been underway, with hopes to convert the Baths into a concert hall and retain it as a cornerstone of the local community.

Ellen Brown

The Empire Pool, Wembley

Location: Wembley, London
Designed by: Sir Owen Williams
Opened: 1934
Listed: Grade II

When constructed, this vast concrete structure, designed for the Empire Games of 1934, was the largest indoor swimming pool in the world, costing £150,000. Williams's innovative structure created an uninterrupted space housing an adaptable 61 × 18-metre (200 × 60-foot) swimming pool compete with 10-metre diving platform, and space for 7,000 spectators. It served its original purpose for only five public summer seasons before being converted into an arena for ice hockey, dancing, ice skating and boxing events. In 1948 the mothballed pool was resurrected to host the 1948 London Olympics aquatic events – the first time an indoor venue had been used.

Thereafter it has provided a multipurpose sporting and entertainment arena, now mainly used for rock concerts, but the original pool is still there beneath the boarding. Originally built by a private company, it stands proud adjacent to the modern Wembley Stadium, having outlasted its original neighbour.

Ian Gordon

LIDOS

Swimming attracts people who don't participate in other sports. Solitary even when competitive, it is hardly a sport at all, rather a contemplative activity, in which surroundings play an important part. Running is similar but involves very little fixed equipment. Swimming, by contrast needs a big investment to provide physical facilities for swimmers unless they are lucky enough to have access to untamed water.

The term 'lido', borrowed from the Adriatic beach close to Venice beloved of interwar film stars, was never clearly defined, and not always used as part of the name, but generally denoted something more than just a pool, often including a café and sunbathing spaces, along with changing rooms and toilets. In 1930, the name was given to the bathing station on the Serpentine in Hyde Park in London, known with pleasing alliteration, as 'Lansbury's Lido' after the Labour Minister of Works who commissioned it. This formalization of a popular but previously 'wild' bathing place was typically one of the motives for creating lidos in the interwar decades, whether at the seaside, where the difficulties of tides and rocks could be avoided, or in cities where the earlier use of lakes in parks was deemed unsafe and in need of control. Other motives were equally compelling – the health benefits of sunlight were being scientifically discovered and there was a drive to involve a wider population in sharing them. In holiday places, a lido was an important investment for attracting visitors. Involving men and women alike, at little personal cost, the lido was also seen as a social leveller.

There were earlier precedents for architecturally embellished outdoor swimming. Cleveland Pools in Bath is an exceptional survival from 1815, a private venture until the 1890s, filled with water from the River Avon, with a simple curving classical building. Recently restored for use, it reopened in 2022 following a 30-year campaign. There are a few other nineteenth-century open-air public pools, such as Pells Pool in Lewes (1860) and Cirencester Open Air Pool (1870), but the rate of building activity peaked in the 1930s. The pools were nearly always municipal enterprises, as were indoor pools, developing initially out of the provision of baths and washhouses.

During the 1920s, it was the large-scale, classically designed seaside pools that dominated, like Prestatyn (architects Easton and Robertson, 1923), and Blackpool Open Air Baths of the same year, in which the London County Council also opened its first, much simpler, baths in three of its parks. These were precursors of a slew of new projects in the 1930s across the whole of the British Isles as some warm summers, increased holiday and leisure time for

OPPOSITE Swimmers at 'Lansbury's Lido' diving into the Serpentine in London's Hyde Park.

workers, more appealing swimwear and an acceptance of mixed bathing added further incentives to their use.

There was also an incentive to build larger pools that qualified for various competitions. Diving was a popular novelty that added to the theatricality of the lido experience, and elegant diving platforms were built with deep water below. Of these, sadly few have survived, even where the pools they belonged to are still extant. At the former Purley Way Lido, Croydon, the listed three-tier asymmetrical concrete platform presided for some years over a garden centre and is now dwarfed among blocks of flats.

Much of the attraction of lidos lies in their modernist architectural style, which overtook classicism after 1930, although there were still some more historically inflected styles, such as Peterborough (1936), with its hipped green pantiled roof and copper-capped clocktower. The architectural styles are appropriately fluid, however, as are words used to describe them – 'Deco' is a catch-all that applies as well as anything else.

Since so many of these lidos were municipal enterprises, the Borough Engineer was often named as the designer, and although not technically an architect by training, these officials were often significant figures in their own right, with knowledge of reinforced concrete, which was the dominant

OPPOSITE The sign for Cliftonville Lido at Margate, which awaits rescue.

building material both for the pools and their associated structures. The results tended towards a form of modernism by default, often with a naïve charm and ingenuity when dealing with awkward sites. One of the best from this viewpoint is the Jubilee Pool in Penzance (1935, see page 67), designed by Captain Frank Latham, unusual for its triangular shape based on the rock formations beneath. Broomhill Pool, Ipswich (1938, see page 78), designed by the Borough Engineer, E. McLauchlan, has a pleasant setting in a sloping park.

On the rare occasions when actual architects were employed, they were never figures of national repute, but R. W. H. Jones, the designer of Saltdean Lido (1938, see page 82), deserves to be celebrated for the embracing arms of his poolside structure, giving protection from wind and making a sun trap, while the bull-nosed projection in the centre is often compared to the internationally-renowned De La Warr Pavilion along the coast in Bexhill-on-Sea. In 1987, it was the first lido to be listed, initially at Grade II, upgraded to II* in 2011. E. Prentice Mawson, son of landscape designer Thomas Mawson, was the architect of the thriving Droitwich Spa Pool of 1935, the only inland saltwater pool in Britain. Abandoned in 2000, it came back to life seven years later. Five firms of local architects came together in the design of Peterborough Lido (1936). Notable too was H. A. Rowbotham of the London County Council, designer in the late 1930s of Parliament Hill, Brockwell Park and London Fields lidos, all in working order, although other Rowbotham lidos have long gone. These are sober brick structures, but remembered with much affection. At Parliament Hill in 2005, a steel tank lining to the original pool reduced the depth, so that the water could be 'turned over' more quickly and economically.

Cold water, even in high summer, is part of the lido experience, but Broomhill was heated when it opened, although the boilers never worked after the Second World War. Woodhall Spa pool in Lincolnshire, also from 1935, is still heated from late March to late September, and rather than Art Deco features, has a giant bath tap in primary colours pouring water into the children's pool, reminiscent of a Claes Oldenburg sculpture. For Londoners, the Oasis in Holborn offers the experience of swimming on a winter's evening amid steaming water in a pool dating from 1946, with an indoor pool alongside on a site where bathing history goes back to the 1730s.

Seaside lidos enjoy beautiful scenery, but pay for the privilege in wear and tear to their structures. Inland lidos have suffered in other ways, through changes in leisure

OPPOSITE Brockwell Lido, in south London designed by H. A. Rowbotham and refurbished by Pollard Thomas Edwards in 2003–7 (above). Jubilee Pool in Penzance, Cornwall (see page 67) designed by Caption Frank Latham (below).

Farewell My Lido: A Thirties Society Report

fashions and their limited seasonal use. A gradual attrition through the post-war period suddenly accelerated in the 1980s, as local council budgets were cut by rate capping ordered from Westminster. The lidos were among the first casualties, often closed for a season, then abandoned in the longer term before facing demolition. In 1991, the Thirties Society, soon to change its name to Twentieth Century Society, led a revival of interest and concern by publishing a report, *Farewell My Lido*, giving historical background, case studies of what had happened to different lidos, and arguing for protection and appreciation. There were several campaigns in progress to protect the use of lidos, and the society played the only card it had by trying to get more listings. We succeeded in 1994 with the Jubilee Pool and a few others, including Tinside (1935, see page 72) in 1998, but there were some sad losses, such as Finchley Lido (1931), with its twin pools.

Launched in August after some hectic weeks of research both in and out of the water, often with empty pools invaded by buddleia, the report came well before the internet made information easy to find. It was a team effort that was rewarded with generous press coverage – editors found that photos of lithe bathers by sparkling water made nice space-fillers on their pages. More significant was a cultural change during the 1990s, especially among younger people, in favour of outdoor swimming, almost regardless of the weather, which is now so widespread that it is hard to remember the repulsion with which this notion was once met. The architectural element, in which the ordinary was touched by the magic of reflected light off water, enhanced the loyalty which certain pools attracted. In addition, there was a growing nostalgia for the culture of municipal services that lidos represented.

What *Farewell My Lido* brought into focus, in succession to the campaign to list red telephone boxes, was the idea that architectural conservation need not only be about artistic value and uniqueness, but also reflected the experiences of all kinds of people, past and present and the use value of certain buildings. This aspect of conservation was recognized in the 2011 Localism Act under the term 'assets of community value'.

Some of the local campaigns were successful in saving their pools, owing to dogged persistence in the face of setbacks, and new models of community ownership and funding were found. A much more complete history and update on the condition of pools was provided by Janet Smith, historian of Tooting Bec Lido (1906), in her book, *Liquid Assets*, published by English Heritage in its 'Played in

OPPOSITE The cover of the *Farewell My Lido* report produced by the Thirties Society in 1991, showing Trentham Park lido in Staffordshire, built in 1935, closed in the late 1970s and demolished in 1986.

Britain' series in 2005. In the directory at the back, the list of 'defunct lidos and open-air pools' numbered 255 in England, 20 in Scotland and 27 in Wales. The equivalent numbers for operating lidos and open-air pools were 92, four and one. There are certainly fewer of them 20 years later, but the wish to preserve them has been maintained. Founded in 2015, the website historicpools.co.uk represents indoor and outdoor pools by sharing information for users and local groups.

Costs can seem prohibitive, yet Westmoreland and Furness Council is spending nearly £5 million on the repair of the listed Grange-over-Sands Lido (1932), closed since 1993, as part of an enhancement of the promenade, although making it swimmable must wait for a second phase. At Penzance, campaigners for the regeneration of the town as a whole saw the Jubilee Pools as a key attraction, so that despite storm damage in 2014 that put it out of action, it reopened two years later, attracting record numbers of visitors. Seeing pictures of tourists in Iceland amid steaming rock pools, European development money was secured to make one corner of the pool geothermally heated throughout the year. Saltdean, which in 2010 was threatened by a redevelopment scheme including 100 flats, is instead coming to the end of a major two-year, £7.5-million upgrade of the fabric in 2024, funded by a partnership of National Heritage Lottery, local council and community support. The dogged persistence of the Broomhill Pool Trust, backed over decades by Ipswich Council, has paid off in 2024 with funds lined up for the completion of works needed for reopening. Although the beautiful Tarlair Pool (1931, see page 46), one of the three surviving lidos in Scotland, has not reopened for swimming, the site was listed by Historic Scotland with support from C20 Society, and ownership was transferred to a Friends group in 2020. In Wales, the sole survivor, Lido Ponty at Pontypridd (the National Lido of Wales, see page 30), was built in 1927 with funding from the Miners' Welfare Fund, and enlarged in 1935, with many original features surviving.

One lido with a fantastic history, awaiting a Sleeping Beauty rescue, is Cliftonville, adjacent to Margate (1927), built in a Hispanic style on top of a late Georgian Clifton Baths complex cut into the cliffside and still surviving out of view. Closed since the 1970s (Tracey Emin was one of the last generation of swimmers there), it represents the last great challenge for seemingly impossible historic buildings in Margate after the Dreamland Amusement Park and the Dreamland Cinema.

Alan Powers

OPPOSITE The giant bath tap at Woodhall Spa pool (1935) in Lincolnshire.

Royal Birkdale Golf Clubhouse

Location: Southport, Lancashire
Designed by: George E. Tonge
Opened: 1935

As a regular host of The Open since 1954, Royal Birkdale's Art Deco clubhouse has become instantly recognizable to golfers. The competition for a new clubhouse by the 18th green was won by local architect Tonge, designer of many cinemas and theatres, including The Garrick in Southport. He said: 'I imagined the lines of a liner at sea; the perfect balance of the ship at whatever angle and from whatever side it was seen.'

The first-floor dining room and elegant lounges, once including rooms for cards, smoking and billiards, have extensive windows giving panoramic views to the west over the course and out to sea. Originally, railings around the first-floor deck and clock tower made it look even more like a liner; these were removed for safety reasons in the 1960s, and the building has since been extended. Tonge's design directly influenced the clubhouse at Childwall, Liverpool (A. E. Shennan, 1938).

Susannah Charlton

Jubilee Pool

Location: Penzance, Cornwall
Designed by: Captain Frank Latham, Borough Engineer
Opened: 1935
Listed: Grade II

St Anthony's Garden and Jubilee Pool were both designed by imaginative Borough Engineer Frank Latham, as part of a slum-clearance scheme. Magnificently sited with views to St Michael's Mount, the gardens resemble a ship ploughing through the sea, the streamlined lido the shape of 'a seagull alighting on the water.' Filled with seawater, its crisp white walls extend beyond the rocks at the end of the town's promenade and embrace the eighteenth-century battery and later war memorial. Sun terraces are animated by 'Cubist' changing cubicles and a shallow children's pool.

    Recent changes include a new café and a geothermal pool. Now at the limits of development, it is part of a unique 1930s ensemble that includes a stylish pub and car showroom. The threat to demolish the showroom – its curvaceous façade acting as the sail of the boat – will diminish the setting and may take some of the wind out of its sails.

Julian Holder

Former Arsenal Stadium (East Stand)

Location: Highbury, London
Designed by: William Binnie
Opened: 1936
Listed: Grade II

The story of the original Arsenal stadium is one of incremental expansion throughout the twentieth century. Founded in 1913, the ground was further developed during the 1930s under Claude Waterlow Ferrier. In 1936 William Binnie oversaw the demolition of the original East Stand and its replacement with a towering Art Deco edifice overlooking Avenell Road. The East Stand is constructed with reinforced concrete around a steel frame and faced in bricks, most of which are rendered with cement. The entrance hall contained a bust of Herbert Chapman (manager of Arsenal during the 1920s and 30s) by Jacob Epstein. The listing of the East Stand in 1997 was viewed as an obstacle to further development and the club moved to the Emirates Stadium in 2006, with the old stadium redeveloped into the Highbury Square residential complex. The East Stand was preserved and converted, and the pitch turned into a communal garden.

Joe Mathieson

Tinside Pool (later Lido)

Location: Plymouth, Devon
Designed by: J. Wibberley, Borough Engineer
Opened: 1935
Listed: Grade II

Like swimmers, lidos were built in all shapes and sizes. Tinside is semi-circular, bellying out into Plymouth Sound. The design is similar to the now lost South Bay Bathing Pool in Scarborough (1915). Tinside is also seawater-fed, with the water being filtered and treated. Perimeter jetties and stepped terraces maintained a connection to the sea, and to the west, there were three tidal pools and a diving tower, all now gone.

As with so many lidos, cheap overseas holidays led to the pool closing in 1992 and it was left to the mercy of the sea. A lifeline came when the Tinside Action Group, with the support of English Heritage, C20 Society and SAVE, delivered 72,000 signatures to Downing Street and Buckingham Palace. The pool was subsequently listed and reopened in 2003 following restoration. Twenty-one years later, further works have commenced which will now secure the future of one of the nation's finest Art Deco pools.

Chris Romer-Lee

Mounts Baths Leisure Centre

Location: Upper Mounts, Northamptonshire
Designed by: J. C. Prestwich & Sons, Leigh
Opened: 1936
Listed: Grade II

Part of a bigger civic centre, Northampton's public baths owe much to the involvement of W. J. Bassett-Lowke, of the Design and Industries Association, whose own Northampton homes were the work of Charles Rennie Mackintosh and Peter Behrens. Dressed externally in ashlared Bath stone, the interiors, including Turkish and slipper baths, were clad in black and ivory tiles, Cullamix renders and Vitrolite, with Art Deco panels designed by Northampton's School of Arts and Crafts. But the centrepiece remains the cathedral-like pool hall, formed by eight concrete parabolic arches. Based in Leigh, architect Ernest Prestwich had no doubt studied earlier iterations of these arches at the Royal Horticultural Halls, Westminster (1928), and Smethwick Baths (1933). He also followed new Ministry of Health guidance by placing changing cubicles in adjacent corridors rather than poolside (as had been the norm), thereby requiring swimmers to enter the pool via 'cleansing rooms', with showers and footbaths, as we still do today.

Simon Inglis

Davyhulme Park Golf Club

Location: Gleneagles Lane, Flixton, Trafford, Greater Manchester
Designed by: Alfred E. McCutcheon with A. N. Potter
Opened: 1937
Listed: Locally listed

There are precious few modernist buildings in the north-west of England. Davyhulme Park Golf Club is a rare example that was invested with modernity from its inception. The committee wished to outdo all the facilities they visited while developing the brief and its contemporary styling was met with comprehensive facilities. Potter was an architect and member of the club and McCutcheon an Irish-born local practitioner. Its curved, terraced pavilion and stair tower are classic motifs of the period and owe more than a nod to the work of émigré architects. Its flat roofs were optimistically described as offering 'a quiet sunny spot for cogitating on a missed putt'. Alternatively, the terrace provided commanding views across the course, its southerly aspect fulfilling aspirations for airiness and lightness. Despite ubiquitous UPVC, the exterior remains in good condition and additions are discrete and remote. As a private establishment, this remains a hidden gem.

Richard Brook

Former Polytechnic Stadium

Location: Hartington Road, Chiswick, London
Designed by: Joseph Addison
Opened: 1938
Listed: Grade II

One of the first stadia in London to utilize the advantages of reinforced concrete, this was designed by Joseph Addison, Head of the Architecture Department at Regent Street Polytechnic (now University of Westminster), which was a major centre of architectural education. Its most astonishing feature is its 9-metre (30-foot) projecting canopy over the lower seating deck. It was used for trials at the London Olympics in 1948 and as the finishing point of the 'Polytechnic' Marathon from 1938–72, the precursor of the London Marathon.

Today, sadly, it is not used, has lost its wooden seating and is closely hemmed in by gym facilities. However, two of the original entrance signs survive: one at the main road entrance, the other in Cavendish Road marking a former pedestrian entry, close to Chiswick Railway Station. A planning application was submitted in 2023 to Hounslow for the site, promising repairs to the stadium.

Robert Drake

Broomhill Pool

Location: Ipswich, Suffolk
Designed by: E. McLauchlan, Borough Engineer
Opened: 1938
Listed: Grade II

Since 1938, Broomhill Pool has enhanced a park in the inner suburbs with its entrance pavilion, plus terraces for sunbathing and watching competitions providing modest but perfectly pitched architecture. Designed by Borough Engineer E. McLauchlan, it was listed in 2001 in tandem with the branch library, designed to double as a wartime decontamination centre. A water aerating fountain faces you as you come up the steps towards the pool, and the original Wicksteed diving platform. Historically, the pool had heating and underwater lighting, although these were lost during the Second World War.

Closed as an economy in the early 1990s, then reopened by Ipswich Council, Broomhill shut once again for repairs in 2002. The 'Sleeping Beauty' may soon reawaken; partnership with Fusion Leisure was delayed by Covid, but the Broomhill Pool Group has secured National Heritage Lottery funding, backed by Ipswich Council, and sounds of happy splashing should return once more.

Alan Powers

Swedish Dance Theatre/Gymnasium for the English Gymnastics Society

Location: St Alban's Court, Nonington, Kent
Designed by: Jocelyn Adburgham
Opened: 1938
Listed: Grade II

Architect-planner Jocelyn Adburgham's timber gymnasium formed part of the campus of the Nonington College of Physical Education. Founded by gymnastics pioneer Gladys Wright to train women specialist sports teachers, the College otherwise occupied a mansion house designed by George Devey (1875–7, Grade I Listed).

At 37 metres (122 feet) long, 15 metres (49 feet) wide and 7.6 metres (25 feet) high, it was acclaimed as the largest timber-frame building in England by *The Architect & Building News*. Costing just under £4,000 and erected in a little over two months, Adburgham's design uses standard timber sections in a variety of European and Empire woods to remarkable effect. Swedish red pine and western red cedar are used externally to clad a white deal frame supported by dramatic triangular buttresses. Internally, the Tasmanian oak floor is a complement to the British Columbian pine used to form her *pièce de résistance*, the Lamella internal roof with a 10.7-metre (35-foot) span.

Elizabeth Darling

Saltdean Lido

Location: The Oval Park, Saltdean, East Sussex
Designed by: R. W. H. Jones
Opened: 1938
Listed: Grade II*

Seaside resorts produced some of the biggest lidos of the interwar era, yet diminutive Saltdean is recognized as one of the best designed. Built to cater for the aspirational new Saltdean Estate near Brighton, the streamlined curved wings hugging its pool provided changing rooms, topped with sun terraces, either side of a circular glazed ballroom raised on slim concrete piers. This central feature curves out to meet the water like the bridge of an ocean liner about to greet the waves, a popular conceit of 1930s seaside Moderne that is particularly well handled here.

Wartime requisitioning was followed by years of dereliction until the lido finally reopened in 1964. Despite being the first lido listed in 1987, its fate looked uncertain until local campaigners fought successfully to save it. Now lovingly restored it is one of only three English seaside lidos still in use.

Kathryn Ferry

Murrayfield Ice Rink

Location: Edinburgh
Designed by: J. B. Dunn & Martin
Completed: 1939
Listed: Category B

One of only a few surviving ice rinks from the period, Murrayfield Ice Rink remains as alluring as ever: a captivating Art Deco façade fronting a simple symmetrical plan. A boom in the popularity of ice hockey and skating paired with improved refrigeration technology spurred this purpose-built venue in Edinburgh. Skating stars Daphne Walker and Freddie Tomlins were scheduled to take part in the opening ceremony of the 'ice palace'. But the building, completed two weeks after the outbreak of the Second World War, was immediately requisitioned as an army depot. The ice rink only served its intended purpose from 1952. Several renovations have enabled the venue's continued use ever since – beside its neighbour, the imposing Murrayfield Stadium, home of the Scottish Rugby Union.

Alborz Dianat

1940–1969

Bon Accord Baths

Location: Justice Mill Lane, Aberdeen
Designed by: Alexander McRobbie, Aberdeen City Architect's Department
Opened: 1940
Listed: Category B

I learned to swim in Bon Accord Baths, a stern, granite-faced pile executed in a slightly purse-lipped, Scottish municipal version of Art Deco by Alexander McRobbie. Exploiting its steep site, an array of promenade decks and staircases trips down from the entrance through the pool hall to the changing rooms. En route, you could admire the building's graceful, arched concrete structure, its handsome windows, the soaring, five-tier diving platform and the 36.6-metre (120-foot) long pool, invariably churning with bodies.

Described at the time as Britain's 'most up-to-date and artistic public baths', everything was of a piece: glazing, tiling, metalwork and joinery. It all served to choreograph a sense of metropolitan sophistication within the insular milieu of north-east Scotland. A film of the building's opening in 1940 shows local worthies dressed up to the nines, exuding a spirit of wartime defiance. The baths emerged unscathed and went on to be enjoyed by thousands of Aberdonians.

Catherine Slessor

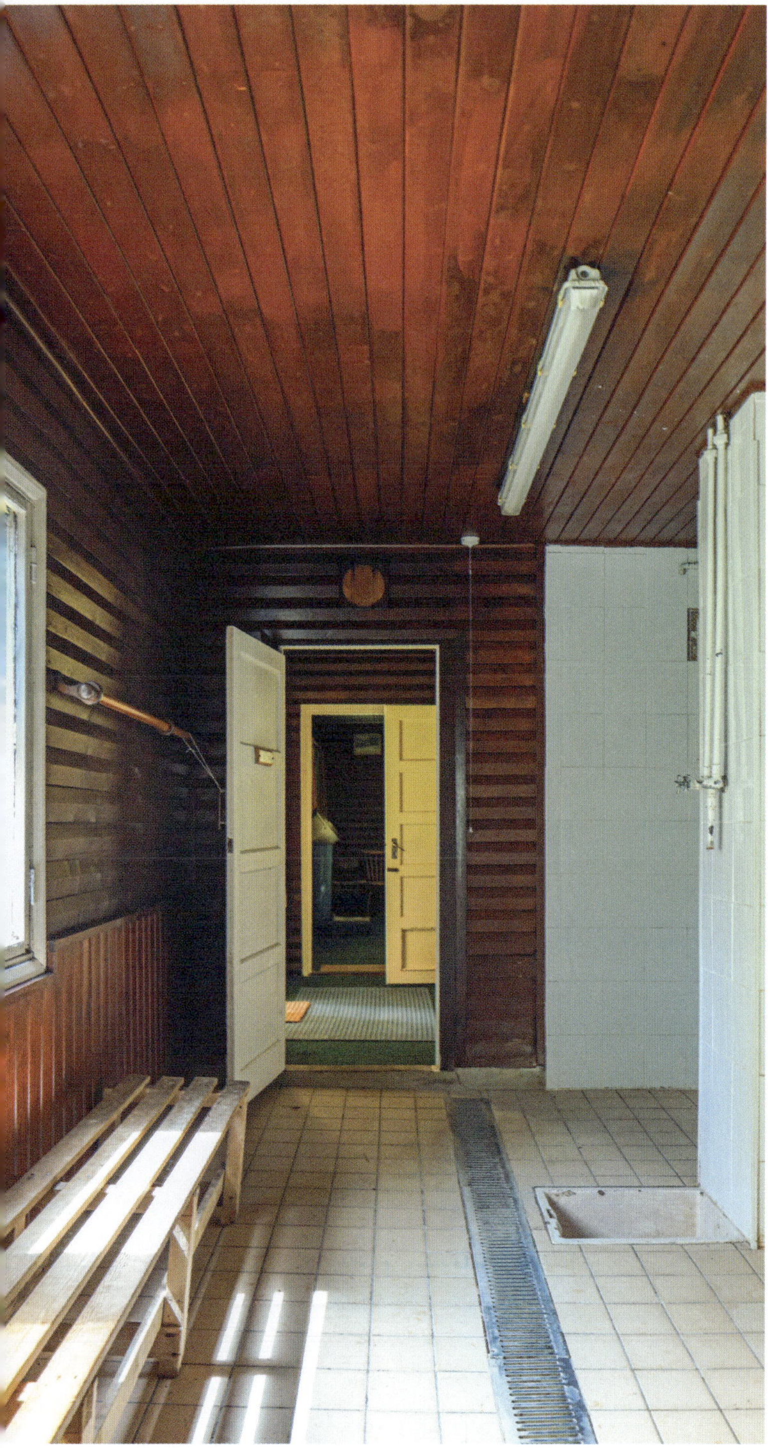

FINNISH SAUNA BATH
IV OLYMPIA
LONDON 1948

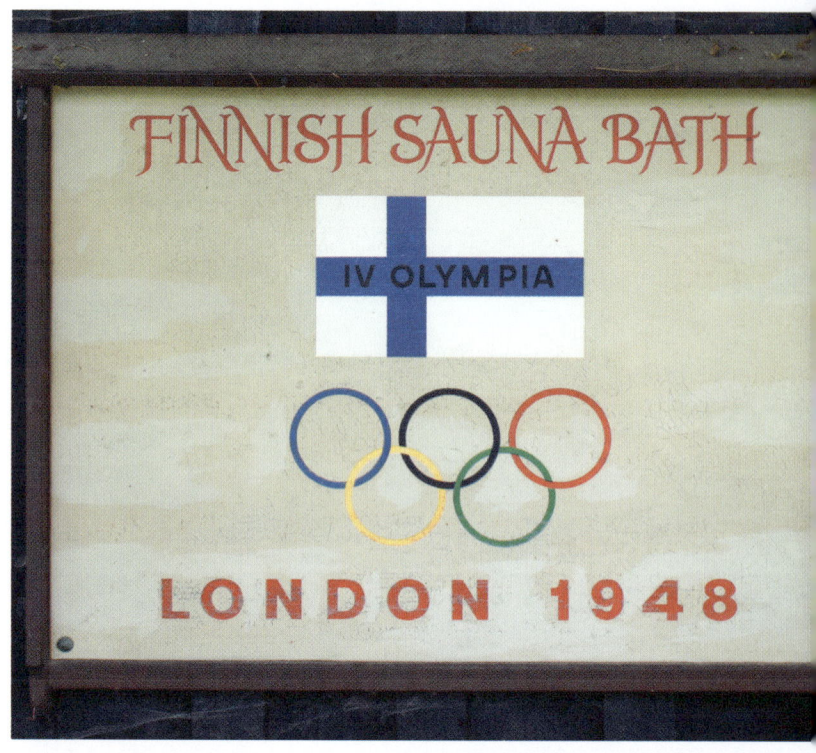

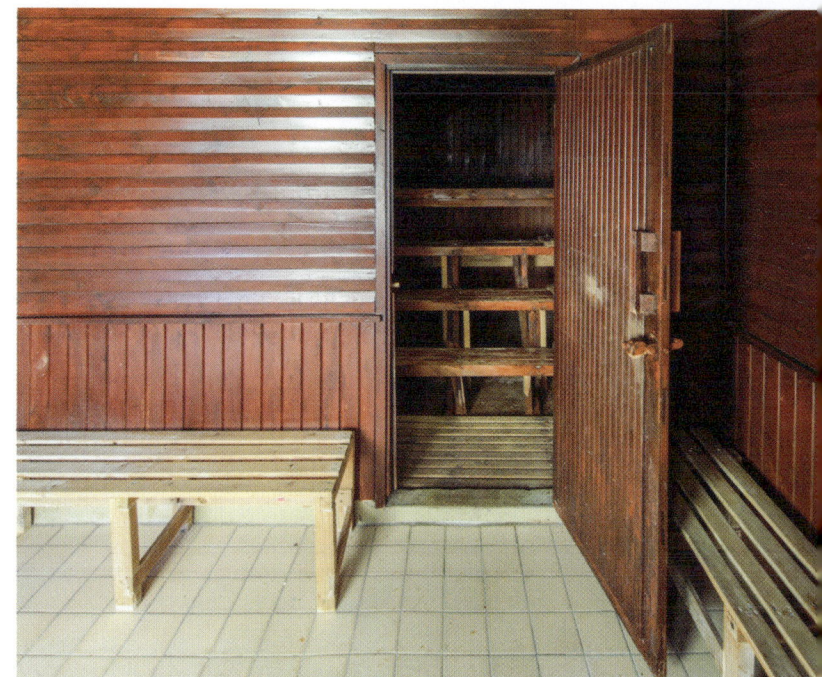

Finnish Olympic Sauna

Location: Aylesford, Kent
Designed by: Toivo Jäntti
Opened: 1948
Listed: Grade II

Post-war austerity meant no new venues were built for the 1948 London Olympic Games. These were mostly held at Wembley Stadium, while some of the male athletes were housed at a former army camp in Richmond Park. Here, Finland provided this prefabricated timber sauna for its team. It was made by Puutalo Oy, a Finnish company that exported many prefab timber buildings to the UK, mostly houses and schools. Later, the Reed paper company bought it and moved it to Aylesford, near their premises in Maidstone.

The sauna survives with almost all its original fixtures and finishes; it's probably the oldest working sauna in the UK, not to mention the oldest Olympic sauna anywhere. A campaign by sauna fans to save it was backed by C20 Society, with the Finnish Ambassador to the UK also paying a visit. It was listed in 2024, and locals hope to repair and reopen it for public use.

David Attwood

Queen Elizabeth II Stadium

Location: Enfield, Greater London
Designed by: Alec Mawson
Opened: 1953
Listed: Grade II

Just off the Great Cambridge Road is the Queen Elizabeth II Stadium, part of a small but perfectly formed streamlined sports ground. The area was redeveloped from the mid-1930s as a recreational complex, with the plans including an oval-shaped lido. The building of the stadium, started in 1939, was interrupted by the Second World War, meaning its finished form harks back to an earlier era of curves and optimism, with a circular brick tower, metal railings and Crittall windows.

Built around a reinforced concrete frame with stock brick infill, metal-framed windows cover half the first floor with the drum staircase tower featuring a curved blue metal stair rail inside. After its opening it was used as an athletics stadium, largely for school competitions, but also for athletes such as Seb Coe, who practised here before his 1984 1500-metre Olympic win. It was refurbished from 2010 and is now home to Enfield Town FC.

Joshua Abbott

Sports Pavilion, Llanrumney

Location: Mendip Road, Llanrumney, Cardiff
Designed by: T. Alwyn Lloyd and Gordon
Opened: 1955

T. Alwyn Lloyd and Alex Gordon were in partnership from 1949 until Lloyd's death in 1960. The sports pavilion is a highlight of their practice, winning the RIBA Bronze Medal for South Wales for the nine years to 1955. Designed to serve the 32-acre (13-hectare) playing fields of the former University College of South Wales and Monmouthshire, and catering for 300 players at any one time, the building is planned as two opposing L-shapes linked together, with easy access for male and female teams (home and visiting) to their separate changing rooms. The first floor includes a large tea room and lounge, around which extends a balcony with a reinforced concrete helical stair giving direct access to the playing fields.

With the site currently being redeveloped as an outdoor sports complex for Cardiff University, Cardiff City FC and the local community, the future of this 1950s gem appears uncertain.

Jonathan Vining

Cardross Golf Clubhouse

Location: Cardross, near Dumbarton, Argyll and Bute
Designed by: Possibly Joseph Weekes
Opened: 1956
Listed: Category B

In May 1941, the Luftwaffe bombed Cardross on the Clyde coast. The Edwardian era golf clubhouse was in military use and was completely destroyed. Materials rationing prioritized houses for repair, so a replacement was not completed until 1956. Its curvaceous Moderne design seemed transposed from the 1930s, featuring semi-circular social spaces with wall-to-wall fenestration overlooking the fairways from a two-storey central block. The architect is unrecorded, but the mid-1940s design may have been by an assistant of the Dumbarton County Architect, Joseph Weekes, who was responsible for drawing up an Art Deco replacement for a nearby farmhouse at Mollandhu, also bombed.

The clubhouse is maintained in excellent condition and makes an appealing aesthetic contribution to its picturesque location. Recently, the club aroused controversy by wanting to install angled solar panels on the flat roof, potentially compromising the horizontal emphasis so important to its design; these have not yet materialized.

Bruce Peter

Boathouse for Corpus Christi and Sidney Sussex Colleges, Cambridge

Location: Cutter Ferry Lane, Cambridge
Designed by: David Roberts
Opened: 1958
Listed: Grade II

Competitive rowing has a long history in Cambridge. College boathouses line the north bank of the Cam: traditionally they were pitched-roofed, balconied, often dormered, capturing the spirit of privileged youth at play. Then the first post-Second World War boathouse broke the mould. It was designed in David Roberts' office and drawn up by Christophe Grillet. Roberts taught in the University School of Architecture from 1946. His early designs were 'stripped traditional' brick buildings: the new boathouse was an advance in style. When completed in 1958, it was the first fully modern building in Cambridge University. It is now also shared by Girton and Wolfson Colleges.

A slender, elegant, symmetrical façade faces the river, masking a single-storey storage shed for racing boats, or 'shells'. The first floor has changing rooms – and that's it. The shed was extended twice, in 1980 and 1990, but the building's original river-facing façade of 1958 remains largely intact, although in need of sensitive restoration.

William Fawcett

Shirley Golf Club

Location: Stratford Road, Shirley, West Midlands
Designed by: John Madin
Opened: 1959

This rare post-war clubhouse has been extensively modified. Of the two sides of John Madin's architectural personality – public/Brutalist, private/Wrightian – this is clearly the latter. Madin, a man of leisure, operates in the Prairie mode of his contemporaneous houses (e.g. Lapworth, 1959) rather than the Brutalism of his public buildings.

Shirley was founded by a breakaway group of Jewish businessmen frustrated with discriminatory blackballing at other clubs. Consequently, budget constraints kept materials simple – brick, plate glass, some dark wood panelling – and nixed a second floor, which members still mourn. An outstanding Wrightian feature is the rustic stone chimney on the southern veranda overlooking the green, interrupting the building's low profile. Inside, a long bar and members' lounge are now semi-permanently subdivided into three smaller rooms. Little of the original structure remains visible outside, encased in new additions since the 1990s. Like many Madins, including many locally, this is unlisted and likely to remain so.

Matthew Bliss

SPORTS STADIUMS

Having acted as a cradle of mass spectator sport in the Victorian era, Britain might have been expected to lead the way in the design of grandstands and stadiums during the twentieth century. By 1914, substantial if mostly rudimentary grounds for football, rugby, cricket and athletics served most parts of urban Britain, complementing the national network of racecourses. (Conversely, a velodrome boom in the 1890s lasted barely a decade.) The 1913 FA Cup Final at Crystal Palace had attracted a record crowd of over 121,000. Glasgow could boast the three largest purpose-built football stadiums in the world. Rugby's showpiece had opened at Twickenham in West London in 1909, while over at White City, in Shepherd's Bush, stood the world's first bespoke Olympic Stadium of the modern era, built in 1908, designed by engineer John James Webster and accommodating 70,000 spectators.

Yet far from building upon these pioneering efforts and continuing to innovate, Britain's sporting infrastructure developed thereafter in a decidedly piecemeal fashion, buoyed by rising attendances (which reached a peak in the late 1940s) and characterized largely by complacence. Compared with their bolder equivalents appearing in countries such as France, Germany and Italy, most British grandstands built for football, rugby and cricket in the 1930s were hardly more technically sophisticated than ones dating from two decades earlier.

As the saying goes, 'If you build it, they will come.' For the most part that is what happened, until finally the creaking edifice started to splinter, with, in football, tragic consequences. Only in the 1990s, following the Hillsborough disaster of April 1989 – the nation's fifth major football stadium incident of the century – can it be said that any sort of meaningful strategy emerged. It is only following the implementation of the Taylor Report, set up to investigate the Hillsborough tragedy, that stadium architecture in Britain can finally be said to have come of age.

To illustrate this, between 1900 and 1939 one designer dominated the football scene. Starting in Glasgow, engineer Archibald Leitch delivered entire grounds, individual stands and terraces for no fewer than 40 clubs. When England staged the World Cup in 1966, six of the eight venues bore his stamp. Yet when it came to designing the new Empire Stadium at Wembley in 1923 – White City having been left to rot after 1918 (one of many examples of strategic failure) – Leitch, then at his peak, was not even consulted. Instead the establishment architect and RIBA President Sir John William Simpson, working with Maxwell Ayrton, was commissioned. Neither had any experience in stadium

ABOVE Twickenham in 1935 – functional, capacious but also 'fearsomely remote from Piccadilly Circus'.

ABOVE The Empire Stadium, Wembley – an international icon and monument to concrete.

design, as became immediately apparent on the near-disastrous day Wembley opened. For all its state-of-the-art concrete detailing – the domed twin towers becoming especially iconic – and later its Grade II status, Wembley's poor sightlines and inadequate concourses blighted its existence until its demolition in 2003.

Elitism unquestionably played a part in Leitch being overlooked. Ayrton subsequently admitted that before designing Wembley he had only ever visited one football ground. Nor did the technical press show interest in professional sport. Where there was coverage it tended to be for sports which boasted an amateur ethos. There was, for example, detailed press coverage of the new Centre Court at Wimbledon in 1922 (see page 16), designed by Charles Stanley Peach, and rightly so. Peach's constrained use of concrete and rigorous internal planning was exemplary. But there was very little for the opening, a year later, of the 80,000 capacity Maine Road by Manchester City.

In fairness, rare was the football club prepared to invest in architectural finesse. Directors wanted to build quickly, to avoid lost revenue during the construction phase, and cheaply. Three exceptions were Rangers (in Glasgow) and Aston Villa (Birmingham), who actively collaborated with Archibald Leitch to deliver outstanding main stands in the 1920s, and Arsenal, whose splendid Art Deco West and East Stands at Highbury, North London, built in 1931 and 1936 respectively, were the work of Claude Waterlow Ferrier and William Binnie. Both Highbury stands survive, albeit as flats, with the East Stand being listed Grade II (see page 68). Otherwise, only three other football structures from before 1939 are listed and remain in use: Leitch's 1905 stand and pavilion at Craven Cottage, Fulham (both Grade II), and his aforementioned imposing red brick and steel South Stand at Ibrox Park, Glasgow (Category B), opened in 1929 (see page 38). Aston Villa's red brick Leitch stand was demolished in 2000.

One tale from the late 1980s says much about sport's status in the design world. As an architectural student at a northern university in 1987, Derek Wilson was informed that as his final degree submission focused on stadium design, he would be failed. 'Stadiums,' he was told in no uncertain terms by the adjudicator, 'were not architecture'. Eight years later, in December 1995, came Wilson's bittersweet revenge, when the Kirklees Stadium in Huddersfield (see page 206), on which he had worked for the Lobb Partnership, was chosen as RIBA's Building of the Year.

For those involved in the stadium industry, the award was a seminal moment. Indeed, the very fact that the term 'stadium industry' had started to gain currency was itself significant, as was the formation, in 1991, of the Football Licensing Authority (FLA). Set up on the recommendation of Lord Justice Taylor, this government-funded body took on the important role of overseeing the licensing work of local authorities, which had been allocated to them under the Safety of Sports Grounds Act 1975 (itself prompted by another disaster, at Ibrox in 1971). Before the FLA, this oversight role had been applied erratically across the country. But just as importantly, having become the Sports Grounds Safety Authority in 2011, it continues to provide a vital forum for expertise and best practice to be shared. Its current chair, ironically, is Derek Wilson.

The Lobb Partnership, meanwhile, would morph into HOK Sport, before assuming its current identity as Populous, one of the busiest architectural practices currently operating in sport at a global level. In the UK alone since 1990 the practice has designed new stadiums for the Welsh Rugby Union at Cardiff (see page 216), featuring Britain's first retractable roof, and for Arsenal and Tottenham, in addition to forming part of the World Stadium Team, along with Foster + Partners, responsible for the new Wembley Stadium (see page 230).

Significantly, Lobb had entered the field in the 1970s by teaming up with engineers Jan Bobrowski to design stands at Goodwood and Cheltenham racecourses, and at Twickenham in 1981. Indeed, throughout the twentieth century and before, if seeking innovation in grandstand design, racecourses were the likeliest destination. Britain's first grandstand specialist had been the renowned Yorkshire master builder, John Carr in the eighteenth century, starting at York in 1753. It was in horse racing that the first column-free grandstands started to appear, in France, at Tremblay (1906) and Deauville (1919). In Britain, engineer Oscar Faber led the way, most elegantly at Northolt Park Racecourse in West London in 1929, where two of six stands built, albeit relatively small in scale – the largest was 19 metres (62 feet) deep – featured cantilevered roofs. No doubt Faber had been emboldened, or perhaps embittered by his experience, three years earlier, of working with the eminent architect Sir Herbert Baker, a RIBA Gold Medallist, on the 'Grandstand' at Lord's Cricket Ground; arguably the most inept stand design of the interwar period. 'Never in the history of cricket has so large a stand held so few people,' was the caustic appraisal of the MCC's Pelham Warner.

Following Northolt, in 1930 another cantilevered reinforced concrete stand appeared at Summers Lane, Finchley, this one, unusually, being double sided, serving football on one side and rugby on the other. Now Grade II listed and attributed to local borough engineer, Percival

OPPOSITE Cheltenham in 2015 – racecourse developments have set the pace in sporting architecture since the eighteenth century.

T. Harrison, it is likely that its concrete design work had been the work of Sir Owen Williams. Williams had earlier worked on Wembley Stadium and would go on to mastermind the trailblazing Empire Pool in 1934, now the Wembley Arena (see page 54). In 1936, an even more daring concrete cantilevered roof was erected at the Portobello Bathing Pool near Edinburgh, by the City Engineer William Macartney and assistant Ion Warner. By comparison, the first column-free grandstands to appear at British football grounds, both steel-framed, did not appear until 1958, at Scunthorpe (demolished 1988), followed in 1961 by the much larger, 10,000 capacity North Stand at Hillsborough (see page 114), designed by Husband & Co. Tellingly, this latter stand was the only football structure deemed worthy of a mention by Nikolaus Pevsner in his entire *Buildings of England* series. Still in use today, the Hillsborough stand remains a modern classic.

Racecourse architecture continued to set standards throughout the twentieth century, as might be expected of a sport which has traditionally enjoyed support from the upper echelons of society, the royal family included. Said to be the largest in the world at the time, Epsom's new stand in 1927, co-designed by Elcock & Sutcliffe and Reeve & Reeve, measured 705 feet (215 metres) in length and accommodated 20,000 spectators in three sections, with

OPPOSITE Liverpool's expanded Anfield embodies football's dominance over the landscape.

cantilevered balconies on its western flank and a range of private boxes. Once again, it would be decades before such boxes appeared at football grounds. Ernest Atherden, of Mather & Nutter architects, who had just completed a stand at Castle Irwell Racecourse in Salford in 1961, sold the idea of boxes to the directors at Manchester United when commissioned to design a new cantilevered stand at Old Trafford, completed in 1965.

Over the next two decades, Mather & Nutter, which has since evolved into AFL Architects – one of several stadium specialist firms to emerge in Britain since the 1960s – would develop their Old Trafford template to build similar stands at Tottenham, Nottingham Forest and Wolverhampton. Each had upper and lower tiers divided by a mid-level consisting entirely of what were now known as 'executive boxes' (or 'skyboxes' in the USA). But in each case the stand costs spiralled, thereby reinforcing the widely held view among football club directors that the very notion of 'architecture' equated with extravagance. Sceptics particularly cited the experience of Chelsea, whose £2 million three-tier East Stand, designed by Darbourne & Dark, opened after long delays in 1974. Although much praised by the architectural press, the stand suffered from a number of deficiencies and almost crippled the club. The die was cast, nevertheless. Wolverhampton's new stand incorporated offices and rooms rented out to a local college. Hospitality lounges started to expand. The complete reconstructions of both Twickenham and Wembley were largely financed from advanced corporate sales and debenture packages. Even in the lower realms of football, and in rugby union and rugby league, a grandstand was no longer simply a platform for viewing. Its facilities had to yield income on a daily basis.

Understandably, economic pressures and the imperative to modernize since the Hillsborough disaster has led to the majority of sports clubs choosing, as they once did with Archibald Leitch, to rank experience and affordability over style. Hence a cost-effective blueprint for new stadiums laid down by the Miller Partnership from Glasgow was to prove extremely popular post-Taylor. Miller had cut their teeth working with the engineers Thorburn & Partners on the transformation of Ibrox Park into Britain's first purpose-built all-seater stadium in 1978–81 – a radical transformation that had been driven by the 1971 disaster. Further commissions followed at Millwall, Middlesbrough, Derby, Southampton, Stoke, Leicester, Hull and Coventry. To many observers, the results may be considered generic, even bland. But their functionality and modular

OPPOSITE Darbourne & Darke's East Stand at Chelsea Football Club, Stamford Bridge (above). St James' Park, Newcastle (below).

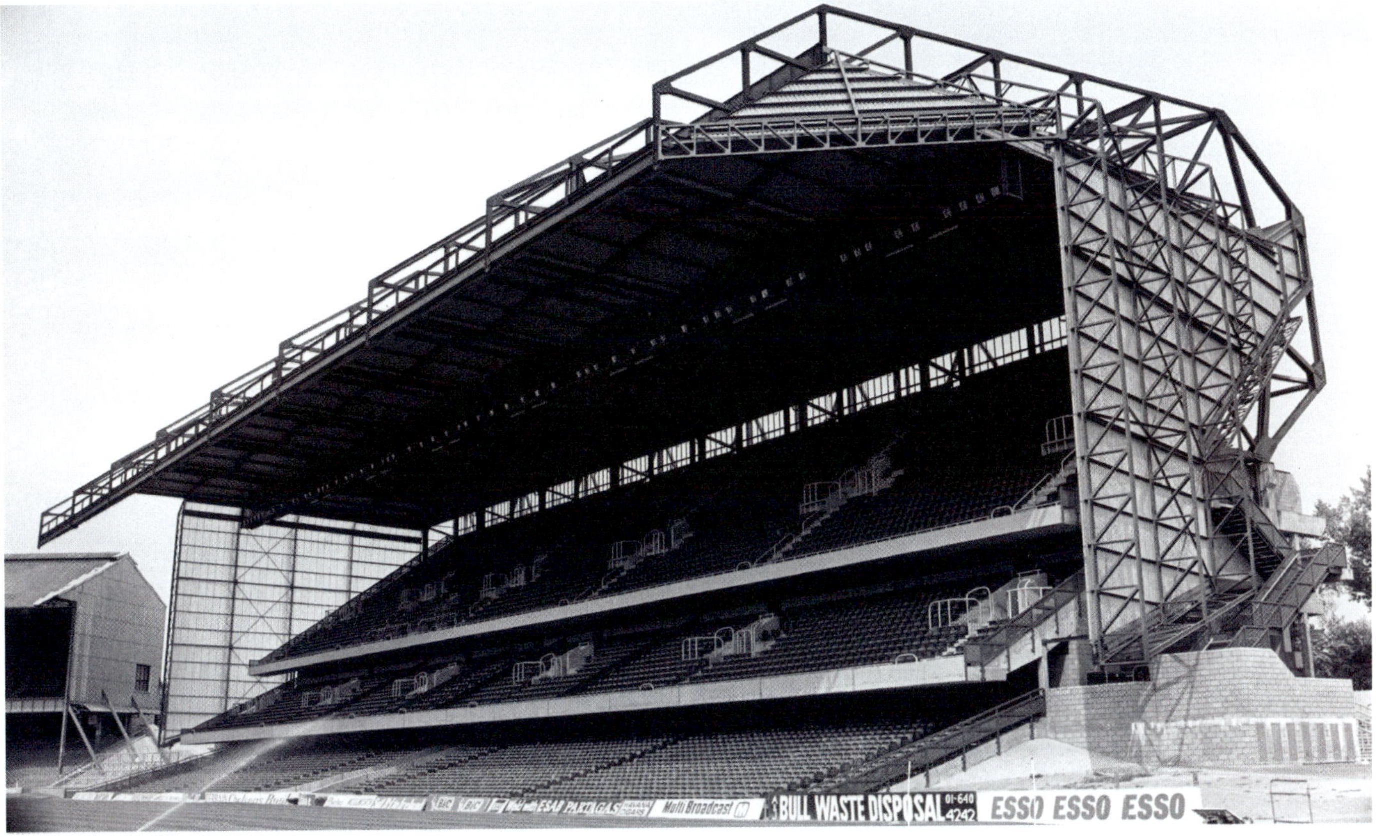
Multi Broadcast
BULL WASTE DISPOSAL
01-640
4242
ESSO ESSO ESSO

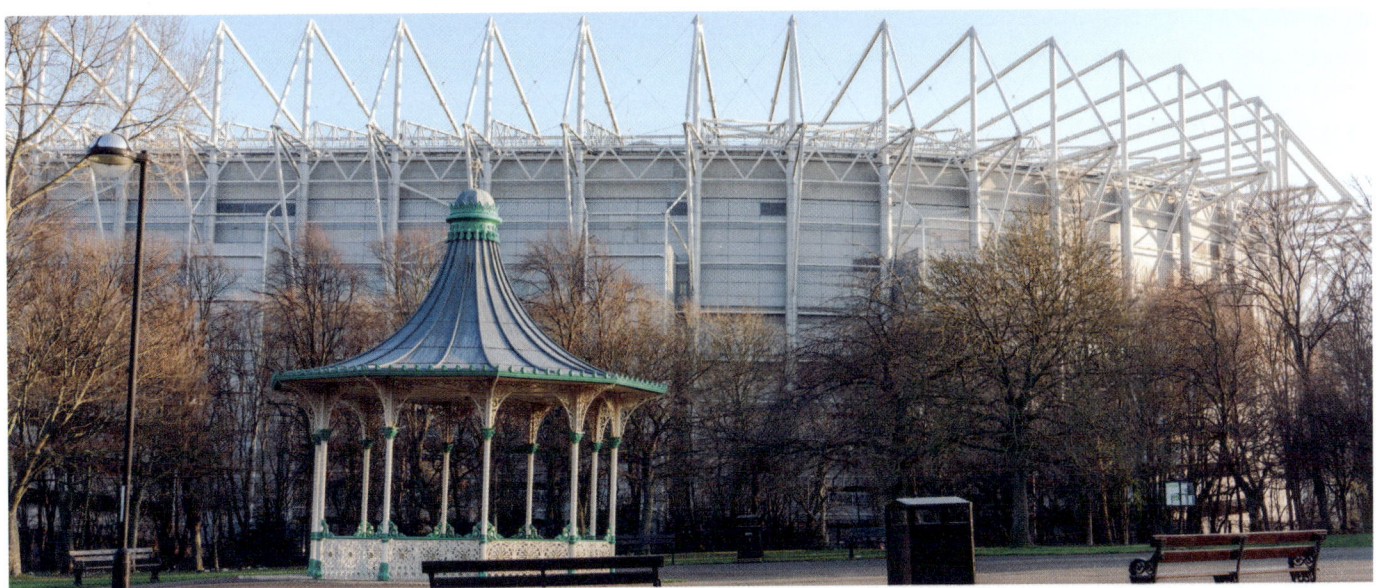

construction perfectly suited the demands of clubs caught out by the Taylor Report.

To achieve viability in this new climate, multi-functionality is now an absolute prerequisite, in the stands if not on the pitch – there has never been football at Twickenham, although increasingly there is rugby at football grounds. So designers must also consider a whole range of facilities which drive up costs by expanding footprints and placing further burdens on building services: extra toilets (particularly for sport's growing female audience), media centres, disabled access, first aid services, restaurants, bars and even sensory rooms. Digital networks and the acoustic demands imposed by concert use have added further to the workload. Also new to the scene is integrated hotel accommodation, as at the Lobb Partnership's stadium for Bolton Wanderers (opened 1997), with rooms offering views of the pitch. This trend has since spread to the club stadiums at Norwich, Milton Keynes, Blackpool and Coventry.

The culmination of all this evolution is perhaps best illustrated in the vast grandstand at Ascot (see page 228). Measuring 370 metres (1,200 feet) in length and accommodating 30,000 spectators, with its 265 boxes, 24 escalators, seven restaurants and cavernous internal spaces, it is on a scale seen only at racetracks in the USA and Hong Kong, China. As one Ascot punter was quoted

ABOVE Tight geometry at Bolton's new stadium reflects British football fans' craving for intimacy.

opening in 2006, 'Why does every new stand have to be designed to look like an airport?' Aside from the obvious answer, concerning the need for safe circulation routes at peak periods, the other response is that this demonstrates that stadiums and grandstands in Britain have finally achieved the status that they merit, and that the teams that design them are just as likely to have worked on airports, or hotels, or shopping malls, but have also recognized the need to understand thoroughly the basic necessities and geometry of spectator accommodation. Modern-day Lord's illustrates the point, offering a truly eclectic ensemble of innovative stands built between 1987 and 2022, the work of Michael Hopkins, Nicholas Grimshaw, Future Systems, Populous and WilkinsonEyre.

Another measure of sporting architecture's increasing public profile is to note that by 1914, the starting date for this book's selection, the majority of British football clubs had settled into the grounds that they would occupy for much of the remainder of the twentieth century. Between 1918 and 1955 only nine League clubs relocated to new grounds, and none between 1955 and 1988. For many clubs, the very notion of a 'stadium' – that is, of a uniform whole, designed and built from scratch, to a masterplan – was simply inapplicable, alien even. (Even now, no one would ever describe Lord's as a stadium.) What the typical British sports club could afford, and what the vast majority of fans seemed happiest with, was a 'ground', a home ground; one that could be developed incrementally, stand by stand, terrace by terrace, when the need arose and when the going was good.

The horror of Hillsborough, broadcast on live television, changed that reality forever, heralding a shift in emphasis that re-imagined football fans as paying customers rather than as terrace fodder or potential hooligans, and requiring the construction industry to grasp the nettle. Lord Justice Taylor was only half-joking when he said, in 1990, that he had wanted not so much to prepare English football for the twenty-first century as, quite bluntly, to bring it into line with the twentieth century. The result is that since 1990, in the top four divisions of football in England and Wales, 35 new club stadiums have opened, with more to follow. Meanwhile virtually all existing grounds have been rebuilt, either entirely or in part. From the Kop at Anfield to the Centre Court at Wimbledon, Britain's sporting infrastructure no longer appears inferior to its international rivals. Thankfully, too, students of architecture are no longer failed for choosing stadiums as their passion.

Simon Inglis

Sports Pavilion, Geoffrey Hughes Athletics Ground

Location: University of Liverpool, Merseyside
Designed by: Gerald Beech
Opened: 1961
Listed: Grade II

Designed by Gerald Beech, a graduate and lecturer at the Liverpool School of Architecture, the building comprizes men's changing rooms, clubhouse bar and café, cricket pavilion and a double-facing grandstand. Its three principal components are linked by a covered timber 'promenade deck' at first-floor level and the design is notable for its elegance, the interplay of horizontal and vertical lines and the lack of corner mullions in the main four-storey volume. In 1963, the building received a RIBA Bronze Award and a Civic Trust Award, and it was listed in 1997.

The *University of Liverpool Masterplan Estate Strategy 2026+: Campus Built Heritage*, published in 2018, assigns 'maintain' as the Masterplan proposition for the pavilion. Since then, there is evidence of investment on the grounds, with a new rugby pitch reported in 2023 as well as the refurbishment of the pavilion. By June 2024, though, the grandstand remained fenced off.

Christina Malathouni

North Stand, Hillsborough Stadium

Location: Sheffield, South Yorkshire
Designed by: Husband & Co.
Opened: 1961

To attend a football match before 1960 meant, in most cases, having your view partially blocked by a concrete pillar. Scunthorpe United had a cantilever stand but it only covered the centre of the pitch, so there was understandable excitement when Sheffield Wednesday announced their intention to build a full-length cantilevered roof at their Hillsborough ground.

Construction of the North Stand began late in the summer of 1960 and was complete for the first match of the season the following year. Soaring above 10,000 seats, the roof is supported by 18 steel lattice girders and is covered in lightweight aluminium sheeting. At each end curving, reinforced concrete ramps allow fans step-free access to raised seating and delivery vehicles direct access to higher level hospitality. The stand cost £150,000 at the time of construction and was officially opened in late August 1961 by Sir Stanley Rous, Secretary of the Football Association.

Andrew Jackson

Coventry Central Baths and the Elephant, Coventry Sports and Leisure Centre

Location: Coventry, West Midlands
Designed by: Coventry Central Baths, Michael McLellan and Paul Beney; the Elephant, Granville Lewis
Opened: Coventry Central Baths, 1966; the Elephant, 1976
Listed: Coventry Central Baths, Grade II

These two joined but distinct buildings were the creative and ambitious responses of the Coventry City Architect's Department to the requirements of post-war municipal sports and leisure provision.

The sleek, steel-framed and brick-clad baths, with their signature butterfly roof and extensively glazed south and east elevations, contrast starkly with the asymmetric, almost-windowless, zinc-clad exterior of the adjacent indoor centre, concrete and steel-framed, the vertical seams erupting into triangles to the northwest. The massive form of the centre, raised on seven concrete 'legs' and connected by an enclosed 'trunk' to the baths led to its nickname, which also referenced the elephant and castle symbol of Coventry city. The baths include a 50-metre length, Olympic-sized pool, while the uses of the centre have included bowls, skating, shooting sports, climbing, football, basketball, dancing and wrestling.

Closed and unoccupied since 2020, the structural integrity of the buildings appears satisfactory, though various re-use proposals have proved unviable.

Adam Dean

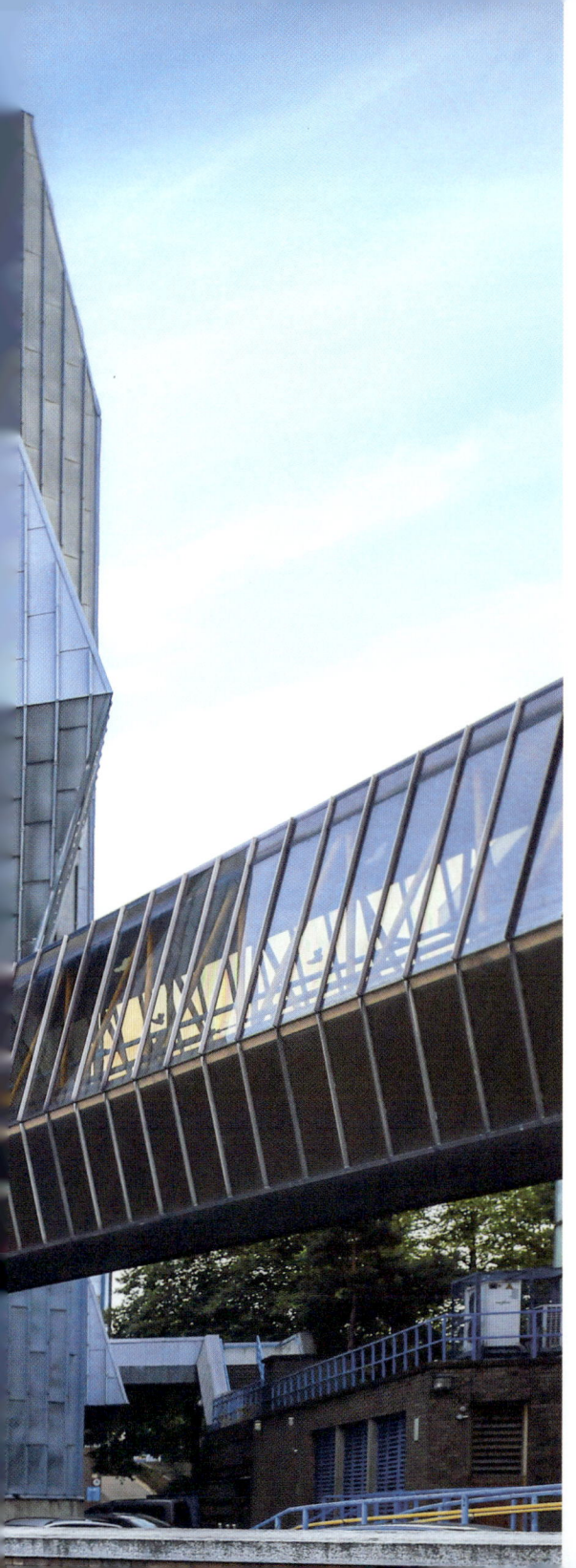

Dam Park Stadium

Location: Ayr, South Ayrshire
Designed by: Maurice Hickey
Opened: 1963
Listed: Category B

Not that special in some ways: conventional modernist ancillary accommodation holding the whole thing up, and some quite ungainly concrete piers. But there is a nice pair of concrete flying stairs, and they lead up to a great open wedge, a straight sweep of seating topped by a massive, cantilevered roof, all as if carved from a single block of concrete. No frills, none of the finesse of Peter Womersley's football stand at Galashiels (1964, see page 124), but powerful and memorable, nonetheless.

The listing calls it Brutalist – and it's certainly of the right period for that – but I can't help feeling there's also a feel of that earlier concrete master, Owen Williams, in the bluff directness of the design. It has been taken over by the local rugby club after becoming surplus to local authority athletics requirements, so perhaps the architectural ruggedness now fits its use.

Euan McCulloch

Cricket Pavilion, Jesmond Cricket Ground

Location: Jesmond, Newcastle upon Tyne, Northumberland
Designed by: L. J. Couves & Partners
Opened: 1963

Opened in 1888, Jesmond Cricket Ground was taken over by Northumberland County Cricket Club in 1897, along with its wooden, Swiss chalet-style pavilion from 1887. This antiquated structure, originally from a local exhibition, was replaced during 1962–3 by the present pavilion, costing £25,000 and designed by the local firm L. J. Couves & Partners, whose founder played for Northumberland in the 1920s. Lightly modernist and timber-clad, while retaining the traditional clock on its frontage, its sweeping balcony provides uninterrupted views across the ground.

A financial crisis in 2003 saw the ground narrowly avoid closure, thanks to a campaign supported by the many international stars and touring sides which had played at Jesmond. In 2006, the lease was taken on by the city's Royal Grammar School, and the newly formed Newcastle Cricket Club was established there. The Jesmond ground remains a thriving community base, its elegant pavilion largely unaltered externally.

Lynn Pearson

Gala Fairydean Football Club Stand

Location: Galashiels, Scottish Borders
Designed by: Peter Womersley
Opened: 1964
Listed: Category A

Modern architecture of this outstanding quality is quite unexpected in the Scottish Border towns. Built for an amateur football club and funded largely by a weekly lottery, this building's extraordinary structural expression recalls the work of Pier Luigi Nervi yet it is diminutive, seating only 620 spectators. Engineered by Tom Ridley of Ove Arup, Edinburgh, it is, in section, a composition of 30- and 60-degree angles, with a 7.8-metre (25½-foot) oversailing roof-canopy supported on four tapering, triangular columns. Constructed in reinforced concrete, its board-marking based on the 12-centimetre (4¾-inch) width of the Douglas fir shuttering planks, the 36.6-metre (120-foot) long stand is flanked at either end by turnstiles set beneath inverted square concrete pyramids. Later reorganization of the ground-floor changing rooms and offices has disfigured its external wall, but recent concrete repair work by Narro Associates and Reiach and Hall Architects has restored the upper part of the building to its original appearance.

Neil Jackson

Latymer Upper School Boat House

Location: Hammersmith, London
Designed by: R. Seifert & Partners
Opened: 1964

For those familiar only with the most famous of R. Seifert & Partners office developments, the Latymer Upper School Boat House may seem a surprisingly modest composition. For although the practice was famed, and denigrated, for its series of boldly sculptural concrete office towers of the 1960s, it also designed numerous buildings at a range of scales, for a range of clients, and in a range of stylistic modes. The Latymer Boat House evidences this well; it provided facilities for the school's prestigious rowing club with apartments above. On its completion, the building's upper floors featured continuous bands of glazing separated with timber boarding marking the floor plates – an effect that mixed the Miesian and the appropriately nautical. And yet, unlisted, the boat house has suffered the fate of many of Seifert's larger office schemes: its façades re-glazed and reclad, robbing it of much of its original charm.

Ewan Harrison

Crystal Palace National Recreation Centre

Location: Crystal Palace, London
Designed by: LCC Architect's Department
Opened: 1964
Listed: Grade II*

Recognizing the country's shortage of sports buildings, Sir Gerald Barry, director of the 1951 Festival of Britain, proposed constructing an exhibition hall and national sports centre on the derelict grounds of the former Crystal Palace. Only the latter went ahead.

    The centre was designed in the early 1950s and opened in 1964. The site contained an open-air stadium and running track, anchored by an indoor sports centre with a central concourse separating the building's 'wet' and 'dry' sides. It opened with the first Olympic-sized pool in southern England, a training pool, diving pool and a rare, reinforced concrete diving platform; while the 'dry' side contained a multipurpose sports pitch. The roof is supported by a dynamic exposed concrete frame and its underside is clad in original teak panelling, chosen for its hard-wearing qualities in a building filled with humid pool air. The Centre is England's only Grade II* listed post-war public sports building.

Carlos Finlay

University of Hull Sports Centre

Location: Kingston upon Hull, East Yorkshire
Designed by: Peter Womersley
Opened: 1965
Listed: Grade II

Appointed on the recommendation of Leslie Martin, the University of Hull's consultant architect, Womersley originally intended the sports centre to be part of a much larger complex of related buildings: what was built was just the first phase. The building is arranged around a triple-decker central spine accommodating a tearoom, lecture and seminar rooms, with a viewing gallery overlooking, to either side, the 9-metre (29½-foot) high sports hall and the gymnasium with car parking beneath (now enclosed). These spaces were designed to be flexible. At the end of the spine were two squash courts, to which two more were later added. Engineered by Tom Ridley of Ove Arup, Edinburgh, the roof of the 36 × 18-metre (118 × 59-foot) sports hall has a two-way span supported on parabolic concrete mullions, rising from perimeter concrete screen walls. Set at 99-centimetre (3¼-foot) centres and tapering to just 12 centimetres (4¾ inches) in cross-section at the top, they give the building both scale and monumentality.

Neil Jackson

Walker Activity Dome

Location: Newcastle upon Tyne, Northumberland
Designed by: Williamson, Faulkner-Brown and Partners
Opened: 1965

Newspaper reports announced the arrival of a 'flying saucer' in Newcastle upon Tyne in 1965 – not spotted in the sky but built on the ground. The futuristic Walker Activity Dome, originally known as the Lightfoot Sports Centre, was one of the first facilities built in response to the 1960 Wolfenden Report. The design reflected the report's recommendation for recreational facilities that would welcome and excite local communities. With a diameter of 200 feet (61 metres), the dome was declared the largest in Europe on opening; an appropriately exhilarating design to reflect the period's recreational optimism, as wages increased and working hours were reduced.

Over decades, the dome's original translucent fibreglass cladding has been replaced with metal to avoid glare, while auxiliary facilities expanded the building's footprint. Despite modifications, the flying saucer at the centre continues to offer locals an escape to a world of leisure. Sadly, C20 Society's listing application was rejected.

Alborz Dianat

Richmond Baths

Location: The Old Deer Park, Richmond, Greater London
Designed by: Leslie Gooday with Stanley Weddle, Engineer to Richmond Urban Design Committee, later London Borough of Richmond
Opened: 1966
Listed: Grade II

I learned to swim here, as a pretty untalented member of the Richmond Ladies Swimming Club, a very traditionally named institution operating in a very modern setting. The elegant sequence of spaces and the park setting created high expectations for my future swimming trips – there are indoor and outdoor pools, plenty of spectator seating, and with three sides of the pool hall largely glazed, an abundance of light. The external sunbathing terrace continues internally as a bridge that partially separates the two indoor pools. The complex won a Civic Trust Award in 1967 and, without murals or decorative details, has an admirable austerity.

Architect Lesley Gooday worked on the Festival of Britain boating lake, before setting up his own practice. The house he built for himself (Longwall, in Weybridge, Surrey, 1964–8) is also listed, and shows more evidence of his interest in Frank Lloyd Wright.

Catherine Croft

Billingham Forum

Location: Billingham, County Durham
Designed by: Elder and Lester
Opened: 1967
Listed: Grade II (theatre only)

Billingham expanded significantly after the First World War as a centre for the chemicals industry. The local authority enjoyed strong rates income, spending more than £20 million during the 1950s and 1960s rebuilding the town centre. At the head of a pedestrian precinct, the Forum is a sports and leisure centre, which also includes an exceptionally well-designed theatre. It was conceived in response to the local authority's view that recreation should be an integral part of Billingham's 'design for living', as well as its desire to be recognized as a progressive council.

The ambitious £800,000 centre includes an ice rink and Olympic-sized swimming pool. Externally, the design combines pragmatism with sculptural moments, notably the soaring vault of the ice rink; it has recently been reclad. Internally, views between different spaces were intended to encourage participation. The Forum was much cited by the designers of 1970s leisure centres, informing Stevenage in particular, and remains popular.

Alistair Fair

Canford Cricket Pavilion and Theatre

Location: Canford School, Wimborne, Dorset
Designed by: Robin Noscoe
Opened: 1967

This unique building combines an elevated cricket pavilion with an open-air theatre, back-to-back. The steel, concrete and brick structure, with a butterfly roof, is set in the mature parkland of Canford School, with a Geoffrey Clarke sculptural relief forming the entrance to a natural amphitheatre at the rear. It replaced a 1920s pavilion that had burned down.

Equally unique was the self-appointed 'architect' Robin Noscoe, the school's inspirational Head of Art, whose enthusiasm and energy enlightened several generations of pupils, including the late film-maker Derek Jarman. Noscoe also built his own home, art school and music school, enlisting the help of unsuspecting schoolboys, as 'work experience'! Opened by Maxwell Fry and Jane Drew, with the sculpture unveiled by Princess Margaret, the project had substantial prestige and won a Civic Trust Award. Alas, none of Noscoe's buildings are listed. Shortly before her untimely death, Elain Harwood was intent on securing its future, now uncertain.

Richard Walker

Bell's Sports Centre

Location: Perth
Designed by: John B. Davidson for the Perth Town Council's Architects' Office
Opened: 1968
Listed: Category B

Among the earliest purpose-built sports centres in Scotland, Bell's provides a multipurpose space under a vast dome. Parts of Perth came to a standstill as the 36 laminated timber (glulam) arches for the dome arrived, with streets closed and a police escort. The exposed beams span a diameter of 67 metres (220 feet): the largest in the UK until the Millennium Dome (1999).

Originally clad in translucent fibreglass, natural light proved unsuitable for precision sports. The dome was re-clad in corrugated sheeting, with only an oculus remaining, and various facilities have since been added. The dome has survived a series of disasters: a fire delayed the opening; proximity to the River Tay has resulted in several instances of flooding; and damage was caused in 2023 when a nearby floodgate was apparently left open. It was announced in May 2024 that the centre is to close, and a new use found. Still the dome stands strong.

Alborz Dianat

Dollan Baths (Dollan Aqua Centre)

Location: Brouster Hill, East Kilbride
Designed by: Alexander Buchanan Campbell
Opened: 1968
Listed: Category A

East Kilbride was Scotland's first post-war new town. By the 1960s, there was growing demand for leisure provision, which fell largely to the local authority, rather than the development corporation otherwise responsible for the town's growth. Newly elevated to Burgh status in 1963, East Kilbride's elected council sought to make a statement of their ambitions on a prominent hillside site above the otherwise architecturally low-key town centre.

Glasgow architect Alexander Buchanan Campbell designed a building whose soaring concrete vault and giant buttresses betray the influence of Pier Luigi Nervi; these international parallels were celebrated at the time as evidence of East Kilbride's progressiveness, ambition and success. Next door, Campbell designed a chunky youth centre in a mixture of brick and concrete. The baths, which included a 50-metre (55-yard) pool, were named after Patrick Dollan, first chairman of the development corporation, and, now listed, remain a central focus for the town.

Alistair Fair

Former Civil Service Sports Pavilion

Location: Duke's Meadows, Chiswick, London
Designed by: Adie, Button and Partners
Opened: 1969

Adie, Button and Partners were best known for their innovative Stockwell Bus Garage (1952), built when buses replaced trams in South London. By 1969, George Adie had left the practice but Frederick Button, who had previously worked with Wallis Gilbert as job architect on the Hoover Building and London Country area bus garages, secured work requiring a high degree of technical innovation. These included building the first helical staircase in the UK at the APV Co. factory in Crawley (1956).

Here in Chiswick, there are two helical spiral staircases: one outside, and one inside a matching top-lit conical brick stairwell at the rear, giving access to an octagonal-shaped viewing lounge. It has linked, single-storey changing rooms to the south, allowing more room for hospitality. Button died in 1969 and the practice became known as 'Triad'. Now part of Kings House School, Richmond, the grounds are still used by various organizations for sports activities.

Robert Drake

1970-1989

Wrexham Swimming Pool (Wrexham Waterworld)

Location: Wrexham
Designed by: F. D. Williamson (Williamson Partnership)
Opened: 1970
Listed: Grade II

Part of a new generation of architecturally innovative Local Authority leisure centres, the iconic shape of Wrexham Pool depends entirely on the use of a great hyperbolic paraboloid roof. One of only two (and the earliest) employed in Wales, the 50 × 50-metre (164 × 164-foot) pre-cast and reinforced concrete shell dominates both exterior and interior, its swooping form mimicking the fluidity of water and the arched shape of the human form while swimming or diving. The sheer wall of glazing to the entrance corner adds further drama and allows a tempting glimpse of the fun within. Internally, the highest point houses the diving boards (now flumes), with the training pool below the lowest.

Refurbishment in 1998 led to a Cadw decision to refuse listing on grounds of alteration. With the essential elements of the design intact however, it was resubmitted as part of C20 Society's Leisure Centre campaign in 2022, and has now been listed at Grade II.

Susan Fielding

Royal Commonwealth Pool

Location: 21 Dalkeith Road, Edinburgh
Designed by: Robert Matthew, Johnson-Marshall, RMJM
Opened: 1970
Listed: Category A

Whereas RMJM's output in the late 1950s had tended towards a romantic 'Scottish modernism', by the end of the 1960s a more restrained, pared-back approach had emerged in the practice's public buildings, not least under designer John Richards. At Stirling University, and in other unbuilt projects, a Richard Neutra-esque horizontality now dominated, with terraces and banded windows precisely articulating the elevations, a role once played by the classical column. In the case of this pool – built for the 1970 Commonwealth Games – the low-slung solution did not just demonstrate RMJM's new language of public architecture, but also preserved views to Salisbury Crags behind. Inside, the sloping site was used to good effect to create an elegant spatial sequence, descending from the 'dry' level of the entrance foyer and culminating in the pools themselves. Deceptively simple at first glance, this is a key work of post-war Scottish architecture, now deservedly listed.

Alistair Fair

Sports Pavilion, King Edward VI Grammar School

Location: Manor Road, Stratford-upon-Avon, West Midlands
Designed by: Robert Harvey
Opened: 1971
Listed: Grade II

This exquisite sports pavilion is set in the middle of the playing fields of the Grammar School attended by the architect's children. It is composed of two storeys on a square plan: the ground floor is faced with plum-coloured brick and the first floor is set back with vertical timber and glazed walls, but oversailing as an oriel window (the cricket score booth) to the south-east. It is covered with a metal roof sloping to a central gutter. The pavilion projects to the rear (south-west) with a viewing terrace over with timber balustrade. The texture is notable – bold fascias, rough timbers, serried vents and brick patterning.

Steps down from the north-east lead to ground-floor changing rooms with many original features such as tiles, racks and benches; steps up access the first-floor function space, also quite intact, with island kitchen/servery.

Listed in 2011, consent was granted for some modernization in 2024.

Katriona Byrne

Arnold Palmer Putting Course, Whitby

Location: North Promenade, Whitby, North Yorkshire
Opened: 1971

Crazy golf took America by storm in the 1930s and, after its introduction to the UK, rapidly became a favourite attraction at seaside resorts. With stunning coastal views, Whitby's West Cliff Putting Course was created between the wars and became part of the Arnold Palmer franchise in 1971. A highly successful pro-golfer, Arnold Palmer was one of the first sporting celebrities to understand the value of branding, endorsing a wide range of products and gaining himself legendary status in the process.

His concrete minigolf courses came to Britain in 1965 and for enthusiasts of the game their ledges, bunkers and flat loops are a design classic. At least 48 were built around the country and 16 remain playable. Whitby's nine-hole course features trademark obstacles including the watermill and windmill with moving sails. It has been run by the same family since 1983 and welcomes back return players every year.

Kathryn Ferry

Oasis Leisure Centre

Location: Swindon, Wiltshire
Designed by: Peter Sargent, Senior Partner of Gillinson, Barnett and Partners
Opened: 1976
Listed: Grade II

'A fantasy structure' and 'flying-saucer', according to the RIBA's *Modern Architecture*, this leisure centre's pool area is a great aluminium-framed glazed dome emerging from a grassy berm next to Swindon's train station. The outside is a simple 'skin', wrote Peter Sargent, 'the contents are the heart of the building'. The dome, which accommodates a large free-form swimming pool and a wave machine (state of the art when it was built), connects to what Sargent called the Flexihall, a multipurpose space for sports, creating a 'wet side' and a 'dry side'.

Opened in 1976, the Oasis was built in 1974–5, the boom years of leisure centre provision in the UK. Its architects were leading designers of leisure centres in the 1970s. Not only was it the supposed inspiration for the name of the legendary Manchester Britpop band, but an award-winning scheme that is much loved by the local community.

Coco Whittaker

Concordia Leisure Centre

Location: Cramlington, Northumberland
Designed by: Faulkner-Brown Hendy Watkinson Stonor
Opened: 1977

Concordia Leisure Centre formed a vital addition to the developing new town of Cramlington near Newcastle upon Tyne, dubbed Britain's first private enterprise new town. The design of the leisure centre prioritized efficiency, rejecting the more exuberant but functionally wasteful spaces of earlier centres. While spatially simplistic, the interior provides a striking display of visual elements including exposed steelwork and appropriately nautical portholes. The palm trees which originally bordered the pool are gone, though some plants remain to preserve the intended tropical chic. On opening, the centre could be hired for dances, dinners and even 'Caribbean evenings' complete with barbecues and a steel band. In 1984, *The Times* listed Concordia among pools 'where you can swim away into the future ... more akin to a James Bond film set or something out of Disneyland than to the swimming-baths that some of us remember'. C20 Society submitted it for listing in 2022.

Alborz Dianat

Edinburgh Dome

Location: Malvern St James Girls' School, Worcestershire
Designed by: Michael Godwin, Godwin and Cowper; Consultant Engineers, Oscar Faber and Partners
Opened: 1978
Listed: Grade II

This startling sports hall for the girls' college at Malvern is a reinforced concrete shell constructed using a pioneering Italian technique, whereby liquid cement was poured into a membrane, which was then pneumatically inflated into a dome shape. Large openings were cut into the dome at ground level, and windows and doors set back within them. It took a speedy two weeks to complete the building. Sitting in a tear-shaped pond, the glazing reflected the water inside, and at night interior lighting was reflected outside. The white-painted concrete interior retains many original fixtures, and its provisions were influenced by the pupils, including a social balcony. The exterior was clad in copper c.1985. Completed in 1977, the sports hall was formerly named after the Duke of Edinburgh who opened it in May 1978.

One of only two surviving 'parashell' constructions in the country, demolition was refused in 2006, the building was listed in 2009, and while still in use, now needs repair.

Katriona Byrne

Richard Dunn Sports Centre

Location: Odsal, Bradford, West Yorkshire
Designed: Trevor Skempton, Bradford City Architect's Department
Opened: 1978
Listed: Grade II

The Richard Dunn Sports Centre was designed as a tent-like structure – described by its architect Trevor Skempton as 'Odsal Big Top' – which contained beneath it adaptable and changeable spaces for sporting activities. A remarkable aluminium-clad, steel cable-stayed roof is suspended on steel masts and supported by huge, crossing elliptical concrete arches, creating dramatic sculptural forms; the architectural press at the time picked up on the team's early use of computers to help design the roof.

Built between 1974 and 1978, the new centre represented a 'conscious attempt to create a permanent community landmark', in Skempton's words. Richard Dunn, after whom the centre is named, was a professional heavyweight boxer and Bradford-based scaffolder who helped build the new sports centre: 'A young scaffolder working on the new sports complex', *Building Design* reported in 1978, 'recently took time off – to fight with none other than Muhammad Ali'.

Coco Whittaker

The Rom Skatepark

Location: Hornchurch, Essex
Designed by: Adrian Rolt/G-Force; built by Skate Park Construction Ltd
Opened: 1978
Listed: Grade II

The Rom is the best of a handful of surviving examples of the hundreds of concrete skateparks constructed globally c.1976–81. After researching American precedents, Adrian Rolt and G-Force designed nine UK skateparks during 1978, with varying feature sets. The largest of this series ('Solid Surf' at Harrow also survives), Rom boasts a half-pipe, snake run, slalom run, moguls, large 'performance bowl', keyhole pool and reservoir.

The pool is particularly noteworthy, being modelled on the Skateboard Heaven (San Diego, 1977) skatepark pool, itself based on a local suburban pool, in turn deriving from the Donnell Garden, California, back to the first ever curvilinear pool at the Villa Mairea, Finland, by Alvar Aalto (1939). The Rom has a fearsome reputation among skateboarders and BMX riders, with a similar status to Anfield or Old Trafford for football. Largely unmodified and in poor condition it needs considerable investment to repair its riding surface and community appeal.

Iain Borden

Wolverton Sports Club

Location: Wolverton, Milton Keynes, Buckinghamshire
Designed by: Pierre Botschi
Opened: 1980

In 1972, Milton Keynes Development Corporation (MKDC) asked Swiss architect Pierre Botschi to design a new sports pavilion in Wolverton. Botschi responded to the brief by designing a double-height shell in GRP (glass reinforced plastic), dubbed 'The Pineapple' for the yellow pyramids of its outer structure. While in stark contrast to the nineteenth-century terraced houses of the railway town, the pavilion's bright interiors and mezzanine bar accessed by a spiral staircase evoked MKDC's experimental designs. The use of fibreglass as a building material led the *Architectural Review* to query the building's longevity. By 1980 the Pineapple had come into existence. Following complaints about the cost of the pavilion's maintenance, the shell was sold to a farmer in Somerset, where it survives, and a more conventional red brick building was constructed around the blockwork core. Though short-lived, small details from Botschi's Pineapple pavilion live on – notably, the custard yellow doorhandles to the changing facilities.

Ellen Brown

THE LEISURE CENTRE BOOM

'Waves in the lagoon pool', the Tannoy would announce, cutting across the noise of Sun Centre in Rhyl on the coast of North Wales. The ambient noise in the building has been described by *Architectural Review*'s Lance Wright as being 'like some electronic aviary', which was only partly absorbed by the colourful lozenges that hung from the glazed roof; but 'when you are screaming yourself, fit to burst, you do not notice everyone else is screaming too.'

Touted as a 'twentieth century answer to the seaside pier', the Sun Centre, which opened in 1980, was a phantasmagoria of sights and sounds. Heated to 28°C (82°F) throughout the year, it did its best to recreate a simulacrum of a South Sea palm beach in coastal North Wales. Three curvilinear, blue-tinted, lagoon-shaped pools, designed for relaxation more than swimming, were looked over by café-filled terraces and overflowing with tropical planting. The whole astonishing, introverted world could be observed from the comfort of a moving car, suspended from what was advertized as the world's only internal rooftop monorail. Rhyl, a traditional Victorian seaside resort, was already seeing its customer base being lost to package holidays abroad. The Sun Centre attempted to counter this by promoting 'a very consistent fantasy: to create the beach in protected surroundings provides the opportunity for all day everyday promenading in just a swimsuit, to bathe in the warm surf or just bask under a palm tree sipping real English beer.'

For the architect Peter Sargent, working for the commercial firm Gillinson Barnett & Partners who designed it, the Sun Centre was the culmination of a string of pioneering leisure centres built by the partnership through the 1970s. Gillinson Barnett & Partners were not the only architects working in the field during the 1970s, but they were the most articulate about the ambitions behind the leisure centre boom. Beneath innovatively engineered span structures in a wonderful variety of forms (a pyramid, a dome, a space frame, a hyperbolic paraboloid) leisure centres mixed together ingredients from an international range of influences, including the free-form pools of Mallorca hotels, the structural frames of Japanese Metabolism, wave machines from Germany (although they were a British invention from 1936), and the fantasia and flumes of American theme parks. The leisure centre boom 'didn't just happen', argued Sargent, but came about because of a period of intensive research into international trends:

OPPOSITE The Sun Centre, Rhyl (top) and Coral Reef Waterworld, Bracknell (bottom).

'We spent two or three years gathering information, looking at the future of leisure, travelling – to Japan, Germany, USA (very advanced commercially) – and we formulated *basic* ideas ... We found that German pools (like tiled urinals) offered nothing. The nicest pools are hotel pools – say in Mallorca; they offer what people want. We're very interested in the common touch, in what everybody wants to do rather than just the selected number. We found that people like to go to Spain, so we looked at those pools, and those pools are always free-shaped, they always have moving water, waiters at the side of the pool, palms, shallow water.'

Gillinson Barnett & Partners had started off building entertainment facilities for the private sector, and their projects from the mid-1960s, such as the Merrion Shopping Centre in Leeds or the New Bristol Centre for Mecca Entertainments, included attractions such as ballrooms, discotheques, ice rinks, bowling alleys, restaurants and bars. Architecturally, leisure centres tended to take their cue from this cheap and cheerful modernism of private-sector developers. Nevertheless, architects largely failed to get private developers to finance leisure projects, at least in their more expansive scale. As Peter Sargent said:

'The most important problem our architect will have to face is of course, money. Who is going to pay for his leisure centre? A developer perhaps? Well, if it is bingo or amusement machines, a dance hall, a discotheque or a pub – yes, a developer. But if it is any other kind of leisure then the developer or the leisure operator cannot be interested.' It was a coup therefore, carried out through a slew of pamphlets and projects, to get local authorities to finance leisure centres, so that by 1976 Lance Wright could argue: 'Throughout the 1970s there has been a phenomenal growth in the design and construction of sports and leisure centres. The pace has been frantic, as if every local authority now feels the new facility to be something which it cannot exist without, and like the pocket calculator, it seems essential to modern everyday life.'

The word 'centre' advertized the movement's local authority origin – adding the 'leisure centre' to those bastions of interwar municipal socialism, the health centre, the community centre, the civic centre, and so on. Municipal government had long provided amenities – from parks to public bathhouses to lidos. Leisure centres were an extension and aggrandizement of such older municipal activity, but

OPPOSITE Bletchley Leisure Centre, Milton Keynes (1973), demolished in 2010.

they grew most directly out of the provision of indoor sports centres, with which they often overlapped. Sargent, though, recognized that as only 7 per cent of people could swim 25 metres (80 feet) without a break, something more democratic than a traditional sports centre was needed, and he was proud that the visitors to his buildings were 'more likely to find fat, flabby squash players, juvenile, vigorous five-a-siders and milk-drinking body builders with pallid white skin than bronzed athletes'. What to call these centres was a problem, as Sargent explained:

> 'Sports Centre implies a smell of sweat, hard work and showers with men and women strictly separated and children a nuisance. Recreation Centre sounds like a place you have to attend after a prison sentence. Leisure Centre used to be the best description but that name has been debased by its use as the one-arm bandit emporium in the high street. The Arts Centre is too specific and misunderstood by half the population who think that the standard of performance and appreciation in such centres must be way above their head – if only they knew!'

The 1970s in Britain are often characterized as a moment of crisis for the welfare state, so it is curious to see the developmental state during this period expanding its purview from the traditional areas of health and education into much more nebulous concepts of leisure and free time. The word 'leisure' acted as locus for many of people's optimistic predictions about the continuing trajectory of changes that were perceivable in society, the result of a period of unbroken economic growth, which was presumed to be sustainable. Much of this growth was predicated on a belief that there would be limitless energy provision; energy that would heat the artificial environment of the leisure centre. A foundational text for conceptualising leisure was Michael Dower's 1965 article, 'The Fourth Wave, the Challenge of Leisure'. Its explosive opening paragraph was widely cited:

> 'Three great waves have broken across the face of Britain since 1800. First, the sudden growth of dark industrial towns. Second, the thrusting movement along far-flung railways. Third, the sprawl of car-based suburbs. Now we see, under the guise of a modest word, the surge of a fourth wave, which could be more powerful than all others. The modest word is leisure … Leisure must be given equal weight with housing, schools, factories, hospitals, in the fight for space: nay more, it must be built into all these things.'

Gillinson Barnett & Partners' first client was Whitley Bay, for whom they produced a feasibility study for a vast stepped pyramid, built around a solarium, with viewing platforms and a dizzying array of facilities, of which they boasted: 'Just as Blackpool has its Tower, it was felt that Whitley Bay should have its particular feature.' Although not quite as ambitious, the completed centre opened in 1974, and contained Britain's second completed leisure pool (just missing out to Bletchley Leisure Centre, by Faulkner-Brown Hendy Watkinson Stonor, 1973). This set off a string of projects, many with remarkably grand intentions, and their clients included South Shields, Sunderland, Ayr, Hunstanton, Havering, Rotherham, Swindon and Pudsey.

Faulkner-Brown are the other partnership most associated with the early leisure centre boom. Their Bletchley leisure centre was a galvanized steel space frame pyramid, glazed with double-skin dark-bronze faceted acrylic panels, at the centre of which was its free-form leisure pool, where flush grills around the pool meant that it was contiguous with the surrounding floor, carpeted with a special material impervious to mould. Bletchley included a dazzling array of facilities, from the chic Keyhole bar, with its wire Bertoia chairs, to a municipally run hairdressers.

Bletchley would be the site of many cultural events, from classical concerts by the London Symphony Orchestra, to the Compass Club, which would act as a fulcrum of Milton Keynes's thriving Punk scene. Bletchley Leisure Centre was tragically demolished in 2010, but in the 1980s the firm would design a whole slew of leisure centres with an increasing dose of postmodernist fun, including new centres in the Shetlands, Perth (see page 196) and Doncaster.

By 1994 there were nearly 2,000 sport, recreation and leisure centres in the UK. In 1980 Peter Sargent left Gillinson Barnett & Partners, alongside Mark Potiriadis, to form Sargent and Potiriadis (later S&P). Their Coral Reef, Bracknell (1989), is at least as ambitious as anything built in the 1970s; its large pirate ship replaces sleek modernism with postmodernist fantasy. But other early S&P projects suggest that municipalities were beginning to have to compete more with the private sector for people's leisure time: S&P designed the Treasure Island area for the theme park at Thorpe Park, which had been opened in 1979. The Dutch company Center Parcs opened its first British UK resort in 1987 in Nottinghamshire (see page 192).

In a multitude of ways, the world prophesied by the 1970s leisure centre has not come to pass. A dyspeptic

OPPOSITE Model of Perth Leisure Centre by FaulknerBrowns.

account of Rhyl Sun Centre by Tim Moore in his 2012 book, *You Are Awful (but I love you)*, captures the failed possibilities:

> 'Hence, the Sun Centre, Rhyl's attempt to "bring the seaside inside", opened to great hurrahs in 1980. Permanent summer! Tropical storm effects! Europe's first indoor surfing pool! But even from the outside I could sense the excitement hadn't been sustained. A massive plastic barn, weathered and anonymous, the Sun Centre looked less like a climate controlled aquatic paradise than the sort of place where you might find yourself losing an argument with customer services about a faulty leaf blower … poor Rhyl. They'd drained the civic coffers building this place, only to see its attractions swiftly matched, then trumped, by every other suburban leisure centre in Britain.'

Predictions about free time have proved largely utopian. The idea of artificially heating a huge structure to a tropical temperature looks increasingly ecologically suspect, and in a time of soaring energy costs, financially unviable. The chipping away of municipal funding has also been a disaster for many centres, with Swim England predicting in 2021 that 40 per cent of public pools were at risk of closing by the end of the decade. Rhyl Sun Centre was itself demolished in 2016.

There was a distinct risk that none of the pioneering leisure centres would survive, resulting in the loss of an entire typology. Thankfully Gillinson Barnett & Partners' Oasis Swindon (1976), with its enormous dome and thrilling flumes, was listed at Grade II in 2021, following an impassioned local campaign supported by C20 Society; although at the time of writing it remains closed. Bradford's Richard Dunn Sports Centre (Trevor Skempton, 1978), with its swooping hyperbolic paraboloid roof, and the po-mo-High Tech Doncaster Dome (FaulknerBrowns, 1986–9, see page 198) have also been listed. There is a wealth of other examples that deserve similar protection. In 2022, C20 Society launched its Leisure Centres Campaign, which has highlighted the extraordinary diversity of shapes and styles of leisure centres, as well as the huge affection these buildings retain for these users. Hopefully the fourth wave of leisure (powered by a wave machine of course) hasn't broken just yet.

Otto Saumarez Smith

OPPOSITE Richard Dunn Sports Centre, Bradford and, above, drawing by Trevor Skempton.

March Stand, Goodwood Racecourse

Location: Near Chichester, West Sussex
Designed by: Howard Lobb Partnership; Engineers, Jan Bobrowski and Partners
Opened: 1980

The first public race meeting took place here in 1802, and 'Glorious Goodwood' became a highlight of the summer season. King Edward VII dubbed it 'a garden party with racing tacked on'. A series of stands, spectacularly sited on the crest of the South Downs, provide shelter and excellent views of the action – none more successfully than this elegant example.

Speedy construction was of the essence, so extensive use was made of prefabricated concrete elements – including 11 slender beams, each measuring 35 metres (115 feet) long and weighing 38 tons, which came by rail from the manufacturer in Norwich to Chichester, before being carefully guided the final 5 kilometres (3 miles) along narrow rural roads. Stainless steel cable stays strung from six precast concrete pylons support the beams and ribbed concrete shells. The main frame was erected in just 29 days. *Concrete Quarterly* praised 'Its boldly articulated structure which floats above the lovely Sussex landscape like an elegant parasol.'

Catherine Croft

Livingston Skatepark

Location: Almondside, Livingston, West Lothian
Designed by: Iain Urquhart, Livingston Development Corporation
Opened: 1981
Listed: Category B

Livingston Skatepark was the brainchild of local skateboarder Kenny Omond, who discussed the idea with the new town's development corporation in 1977. The corporation was keen to provide leisure facilities for the town's young population – which, notably, included the expat employees of several American firms. Project architect Iain Urquhart and his wife Dee took the design seriously, spending time visiting skateparks in the USA, Europe and England; Dee Urquhart became a skateboarder herself.

The structure, which also includes a climbing wall, was part-funded by the Scottish Sports Council as an experimental prototype. It demonstrates well the extent to which state funding for sports was responsive to new agendas during the 1970s. Iain Urquhart helped construct the skatepark, using his own specially designed machine to achieve the necessary smooth concrete surfaces. Quickly recognized as a highly successful design and extended several times, it continues to attract visitors from across Scotland and beyond.

Alistair Fair

Plas y Brenin (National Outdoor Centre)

Location: Capel Curig, Conwy
Designed by: Bowen Dann Davies Partnership
Opened: c.1981
Listed: Grade II

The village of Capel Curig – high up in the heart of Eryri National Park – has been a tourist destination since before the eighteenth century. Around 1800, English architect Benjamin Wyatt designed a wayside inn for Lord Penrhyn at the north-eastern edge of Llynnau Mymbyr. George Borrow stayed there in 1854 and described it in his book *Wild Wales* as 'a very magnificent edifice'. It was later re-named the Royal Hotel.

Plas y Brenin was established in 1955 and has subsequently grown to become one of the leading outdoor centres in the UK. In the early 1980s, contemporaneously with Plas Menai (see page 182), the former Royal Hotel was altered and enlarged by Bowen Dann Davies Partnership for the Sports Council (now Sport England) as a mountaineering centre. The deceptively simple extensions are skilfully composed with roughcast rendered walls, natural slate roofs, and the practice's signature crisp timber detailing – modern, yet sympathetic to the late Georgian original.

Jonathan Vining

Woughton Pavilion

Location: Woughton Sports Ground, Milton Keynes, Buckinghamshire
Designed by: Peter Howard for Milton Keynes Development Corporation
Opened: 1981

When it came to producing one-offs for Milton Keynes Development Corporation, they often turned to in-house architect Peter Howard, who designed some of the most eccentric buildings in contrasting styles for the new town. The eclectic historicism of Howard's work feels more influenced by Clough Williams-Ellis's Portmeirion than contemporary postmodernism. There's no reason why this sports pavilion should take the form of a Chinese pagoda with fretted gables and curved layers of roofs, other than that it sparks a whimsical joy in all who use it – despite, perhaps, a slight lack of flexibility for different sports, from cricket to rugby. It has been important to retain the pavilion's colour scheme during maintenance works and attempts to tone it down to black and white have so far been avoided. The rather plain ancillary building, once a caretaker's residence and now a gym, is likely to face pressure to be demolished and replaced.

John Grindrod

Plas Menai (National Outdoor Centre for Wales)

Location: Caernarfon, Gwynedd
Designed by: Bowen Dann Davies Partnership
Opened: 1982
Listed: Grade II*

One of the most architecturally significant Welsh buildings of the late twentieth century, this outdoor centre beside the Menai Strait was built for the Sports Council for Wales (now Sport Wales). It is organized as clusters of accommodation around two half-open courts of different character, providing shelter from the prevailing weather. The building's profile, with its expansive, cascading pitched roofs, echoes the Eryri backdrop to the south and was a key element in integrating what is a substantial building – five storeys in places – into the vista from Anglesey. It won the Gold Medal for Architecture at the National Eisteddfod of Wales in 1985, and a RIBA Commendation in 1986. In 2002, Richard Weston, then a research fellow at the Welsh School of Architecture, wrote that it was 'arguably, the most admired and influential building completed in Wales in the last quarter of a century' and regarded by many 'as the most persuasive built manifesto of the search for a Welsh architecture'.

Jonathan Vining

Oxford Ice Rink

Location: Oxpens Road, Oxford
Designed by: Nicolas Grimshaw and Partners
Opened: 1984

Ice skating has long been enjoyed in Oxford, from races on the flooded Thames in hard winters to a short-lived indoor rink of 1930 at Botley Road. Half a century later, a band of skaters spearheaded by the US-born Mary Meagher launched the Oxford Ice Skating Trust. Amid the World and Olympic successes of Torvill and Dean from 1981, their campaign for a new rink was taken up by Oxford City Council who identified a new site, earmarked funding and commissioned Grimshaw and Partners. The result is perhaps the city's most distinctive instance of High Tech architecture. The twin-masted, long-span structure, ostensibly chosen to minimize piled foundations due to poor ground conditions, lends a touch of drama to what is otherwise a straightforward shed. Since 1984 the rink has been the home of the Oxford City Stars ice hockey team, although it faces an uncertain future as the surrounding Oxpens site undergoes redevelopment.

Geraint Franklin

Brixton Recreation Centre

Location: Brixton, London
Designed by: George Finch, Lambeth Borough Council Architect's Department
Opened: 1985
Listed: Grade II

In 1969, the Greater London Plan proposed a motorway, with a hub in Brixton linking to the A23 to Brighton. In response, Ted Hollamby, Director of Development Services for Lambeth, proposed a radical new town centre, with raised walkways to a recreation centre acting as a central hub. Designed in 1970, this is the first and only implemented phase.

Built over six levels, it incorporates three swimming pools, a main sports hall, a large bowls halls, eight squash courts, gymnasium and facilities for other activities including judo, shooting and cricket as well as a restaurant, a bar, two cafés, a disco, and a caretaker's flat. A climbing wall rises through the top-lit atrium. The list description cites its cultural as well as its architectural importance: as a social centre for the local Black community, visited by Nelson Mandela in 1996. Its monolithic brick masses, and dramatic, sculptural spaces are bold, robust and popular.

Catherine Croft

Henley Royal Regatta Headquarters

Location: Henley-on-Thames, Oxfordshire
Designed by: Terry Farrell Partnership
Opened: 1986
Listed: Grade II

An annual regatta has been held at Henley-on-Thames since 1839. Rowing competitions can be traced to the medieval Venetian *regata* and beyond to ancient Greece and Egypt. This sporting heritage underpins Terry Farrell's historicizing design for the headquarters of the Henley Royal Regatta. It stands at the entrance to the town on a green belt site adjacent to its eighteenth-century bridge. A temple-fronted pavilion accommodating crew room, offices, committee room and a secretary's flat sits upon a broad, battered plinth. At river level is a wet dock and storage for the piles, booms and pontoons, which mark out the racecourse. The central void of the dock is carried up to create the impression of a broken pediment. The building tacks closer to the classical revival than any other Farrell project. The curved sunscreen of the central balcony references the Adelphi, another riverside building, while the rear elevation sports a Venetian window.

Geraint Franklin

Center Parcs

Location: Sherwood Forest, Nottinghamshire
Designed by: Centre Parcs Architects; Consulting Engineers, Ove Arup & Partners; Contractor, John Laing Construction
Opened: 1987

In Sherwood Forest is a Dutch modernist vision of the future: a subtropical swimming pool inside a giant geodesic dome, surrounded by leisure facilities, chalets and pine trees. Center Parcs was founded in 1968 by Dutch businessman Piet Derksen: this was the first in Britain. Artificially heated halls and chalets with log burners extended the holiday season for families, accommodating 3,000 self-catering visitors, 365 days a year. The flamboyant swimming hall has wave machines, spa baths, waterfalls, wild-water rapids, high-level flumes and café, with subtropical landscaping, in a dome 70 metres (230 feet) wide, constructed from laminated timber beams and triple glazed with a translucent PTFE membrane. Transport is by hired bicycles. A network of streams, pools and lakes is operated by pumps. The flat-roofed chalets were built of bespoke concrete blocks in brick sizes to give a sense of domesticity, with a staggered layout for privacy. By 2012 Sherwood Forest had 400,000 visitors per year.

Chris Matthews

Mound Stand, Lord's Cricket Ground

Location: Regent's Park, London
Designed by: Michael Hopkins and Partners
Opened: 1987

The Mound Stand represents the stunning use of High Tech design in a hallowed sporting venue. Completed for the 200th anniversary of the Marylebone Cricket Club, it is celebrated for its innovative use of materials and engineering techniques. Hopkins said that the idea was to evoke a 'tent by the village cricket green' but his approach was far more flamboyant: appropriate for the most famous cricket club in the country. The design features a spectacular tensile roof, supported by cables and merely six steel masts, creating a lightweight yet visually striking structure sitting above a retained and extended brick arcade. The strength of the design is that it provides unobstructed views for spectators, with the clever use of glass and steel allowing natural light to flood the interior, further enhancing the audience experience. It marked a significant evolution in stadium architecture and shows how contemporary design can be integrated into historic contexts.

Clare Price

Perth Leisure Centre

Location: Perth
Designed by: FaulknerBrowns
Opened: 1988

'Perth is one of the new generation of pools that are no longer mere pool halls, but are vibrant social spaces where water is the main medium.' The architects accordingly expressed the intended function of Perth Leisure Centre as a bustling hub for the region, achieved with an array of offerings. The centre provided perhaps the most comprehensive range of swimming facilities ever seen in the United Kingdom, with three pools, an outdoor lagoon, sauna, steam room, spa bath, jacuzzi, novelty showers and solariums. The west elevation dominates the design, with two flumes bursting out above an adjoining bridge beside a semi-circular entrance foyer, glazed to attract passers-by. The steel frame is exposed throughout the interior, providing a striking display of the structure, a hallmark of FaulknerBrowns' designs. The local authority has approved plans to replace the leisure centre, though redevelopment has stalled. The future of this leisure landmark remains uncertain.

Alborz Dianat

The Dome

Location: Doncaster, South Yorkshire
Designed by: FaulknerBrowns
Opened: 1989
Listed: Grade II

Emblematic of the shift of sports centres into tourist landmarks, the Doncaster Dome is one of the largest leisure facilities in the United Kingdom. Throughout the playful arrangement of spaces, postmodern and High Tech trends are interposed in masonry and steel. A glazed rotunda stands at the centre; as Cath Slessor has observed, a 'mock Pantheon dedicated to the gods of leisure'. Among numerous attractions on opening was the largest flume ride in Britain measuring 120 metres (394 feet) long with a free-form ice skating rink.

Previously used for coalmining, the site was repurposed to capitalize on the leisure boom, serving as a catalyst for Doncaster's regeneration. Accommodating functions beyond sport, Engelbert Humperdinck was among artists to perform at the Dome in its opening year, followed by Radiohead, The Prodigy and Ed Sheeran in subsequent decades. The Dome remains almost entirely in its original form, continuing to honour the gods of leisure with myriad amusements.

Alborz Dianat

1990-1999

Ships & Castles Leisure Pool

Location: Falmouth, Cornwall
Designed by: Andrew Robertson & Partners
Opened: 1993

This imposing, elevated fusion structure, mostly metal framed, overlooks Falmouth and was completed for Cornwall Council. Respecting the proximity to Pendennis Castle, the front façade has six crenelated turrets dressed in red/black brick with toothed stone quoins and four buttresses in brick and stone on each side elevation. The pitched roof is slated to ridge height. The contrasting town/seaward side takes advantage of the falling terrain and boasts a magnificent green curved rectangular roof with several double-glazed, self-cleaning units which together resemble a sail. Inside, the castle theme continues with strong marine references in the form of portholes, railings, etc.

A listing application prompted by its closure in March 2022 was sadly refused. The facility was devolved to Falmouth Council in December 2023 and is now managed by a community group called Pendennis Leisure. Plans will soon be submitted to remodel the building with the potential loss of its key features.

Robert Dowden

East Sussex National Golf Clubhouse

Location: Uckfield, East Sussex
Designed by: Michael Blee Whittaker Partnership
Opened: 1994

From afar this golf complex could be a collection of oast houses, as it was designed to echo the local vernacular Wealden architecture. On closer inspection, there is a definite 'po-mo' vibe, but only by taking account of Michael Blee's career can other influences be understood. Blee had a long connection to Sussex, and worked in Sri Lanka with Minette de Silva, who in turn had worked with Le Corbusier. Blee was also a project architect for Basil Spence – whose practice designed Sussex University at the start of the 1960s.

East Sussex National was designed to host professional European tour golf events, but these no longer take place here. Visiting in 2022 parts of the prestigious clubhouse building seemed unused and externally in need of some care. On a positive note, it is a thriving amateur golf venue, and the 2000s hotel includes a rebuilt Wurlitzer organ, which is used for concerts.

Cela Selley

Kirklees Stadium

Location: Huddersfield, West Yorkshire
Designed by: The Lobb Partnership; Engineers, YRM Anthony Hunt
Opened: 1994

Based on their conceptual 'A Stadium for the Nineties', the designers used 3D computer modelling to design this very colourful 25,000 seat stadium that set a new design mould for stadia.

An all-seater in compliance with UK legislation after the 1990 Taylor Report on the Hillsborough disaster in Sheffield, it is relatively intimate, oval in plan, with no seat more than 90 metres (295 feet) from the centre spot. The stands are shaped like orange segments – high and deep at the centre, low and shallow at the extremities – and the roof is supported by banana-shaped prismatic steel trusses. These span up to 143 metres (469 feet) and spring from two pins on massive concrete thrust blocks at the stadium's corners. Each block is held aloft by four smooth concrete legs and carries floodlight masts.

The stadium, currently known as John Smith's Stadium, won the 1995 RIBA Building of the Year. Now refurbishment costing up to £10 million is needed to extend its life to 2050.

Christopher R Marsden

Liverpool Watersports Centre

Location: Queen's Dock, Liverpool, Merseyside
Designed by: Marks Barfield Architects
Opened: 1995

Set in the south-east corner of Queen's Dock, the centre was designed to provide affordable watersports, such as swimming, sailing, kayaking and paddleboarding, for the local community, including inner-city children and people with disabilities. In *Pevsner Architectural Guides Liverpool*, Joseph Sharples describes it as the best building completed under the Merseyside Development Corporation: 'A pavilion visually "floating" in the dock (though actually built on piles), so emphasizing its purpose.' It has an exposed steel frame, with a lower 'wet' pontoon and an upper 'dry' deck supported on trusses, and includes facilities such as offices, changing rooms and a café.

Completed in 1994, and officially opened in 1995, the building won the 1995 RIBA Regional Award, a Structural Steel Design Award and Liverpool Architecture and Design Trust Award. An early work by David Marks and Julia Barfield, it has the structural elegance so notable in the London Eye, which brought these architects to public attention.

Susannah Charlton

Murrayfield Stadium

Location: Roseburn Street, Edinburgh
Designed by: Miller Partnership
Opened: 1994

With rugby union internationals having taken place in Scotland since 1871, the Scottish Rugby Union bought this site in 1925. A new east stand was commissioned in 1979, opposite the 1920s original, as the first phase of total redevelopment. The west, south and north stands followed in the 1990s, their design having been amended in the light of the 1990 Taylor Report on the Hillsborough disaster in order to be fully seated while retaining the planned capacity of 67,000; this is evident in their bigger canopies – 48 metres (157 feet) for the west stand – and more complex circulation. Completed to a tight schedule between seasons and organized as a continuous 'bowl', the stands feature hammered in-situ concrete columns, with other elements in precast concrete and exposed self-weathering steelwork. On clear view are stairs, galleries and hospitality areas. Miller Partnership (now Holmes Miller) became specialists in stadium design, working subsequently at Old Trafford and the Oval.

Alistair Fair

Grace Stand, Towcester Racecourse

Location: Towcester, Northamptonshire
Designed by: Francis Roberts
Opened: 1997

In February 1988, an article in *Country Life* by Roderick Gradidge, a founding Trustee of C20 Society, praised the architecture of St Mary Magdalen at Penwortham near Preston. It was read by Lord Alexander Hesketh, who visited the church and commissioned its architect to design a new grandstand for his small country racecourse at Towcester.

Modern racecourse architecture at the time was generally rather dull – punters naturally being more interested in the horses – so Lord Hesketh's desire for beauty baffled the horse racing fraternity. Roberts' lifelong love of the picturesque and traditional construction, initially a personal stance against High Tech architecture, meant that his plans could often be realized by competent local builders. Skilled artisans were sourced for decorative fittings, such as the lighting at Towcester by a former ship's chandlers. Roberts was later commissioned by Hesketh to design a second grandstand in the same style (pictured above).

Andrew Jackson

Lord's Media Centre

Location: Regent's Park, London
Designed by: Future Systems
Opened: 1999

This highly futuristic, Stirling prize-winning pod accommodates journalists and broadcasters reporting on cricket matches. It was designed by Future Systems – architects known for their bionic, amorphous 'blobitecture'. The centre straddles the Hopkins-designed Compton and Edrich Stands and stands 15 metres (49 feet) in the air, dominating the western end of the ground.

The semi-monocoque, all-aluminium shell was the first of its type in the world and used boat-building technology. It was manufactured by a Dutch shipbuilding company, prefabricated in Cornwall, then taken apart and shipped in sections to London before being rebuilt on site. The fully glazed glass front elevation slopes inwards to its base, in order to eliminate glare and reflection. The upper part has the building's only opening window, installed to allow sound from the ground itself to create atmosphere during broadcasts. Plans for alterations led to an unsuccessful listing application by C20 Society in 2015.

Clare Price

Millennium Stadium (Principality Stadium)

Location: Cardiff
Designed by: Rod Sheard, Lead Architect, Lobb Sports Architecture
Opened: 1999

Replacing the National Stadium, home of Welsh rugby (some might say Welsh national identity), for the 1999 Rugby World Cup was a monumental task, especially given a brief to build 'the most atmospheric rugby stadium in the world'. Creating that atmosphere within the constrictions of a city-centre site fundamentally shaped the innovative design. The steeply raked tiers of seating form a ravine, at once vast and intimate, so every seat holder feels on top of the action. This form and the retractable roof, insulated to increase its acoustic capabilities, makes the sound of 74,000 supporters reverberate unforgettably. At each corner, 90-metre (295-foot) high masts support the superstructure and make the stadium visible in the cityscape. At the north end, a surviving section of its predecessor embeds the memories of rugby past. Also used for concerts and other high-profile sporting events, the stadium quickly became a new symbol of Welsh national pride and hope for the future.

Susan Fielding

2000–present

Xscape

Location: Milton Keynes, Buckinghamshire
Designed by: FaulknerBrowns
Opened: 2000

A classic millennium-era project, like a slice from Richard Rogers' Dome, Xscape is a leisure and retail complex combining the Snozone – a 170-metre (558-foot) long ski slope that uses real snow – above a multiplex cinema, adventure golf, skydiving simulator, bowling lanes and restaurants. For 20 years the towering dome was the second tallest building in Milton Keynes after Mellish Court, Bletchley, the tower block built before the development corporation's rule not to build higher than the tallest tree. The dome shape helps lessen its impact, making it feel more landscape feature than building, helped by the (very Milton Keynes) metallic sheen to the cladding. FaulknerBrowns had previously designed the Archigram-style Bletchley Leisure Centre (1973–2009) for the new town, making their appointment as architects for developers X-Leisure very fitting. Always busy and well used it forms the heart of the new city's nightlife, and its success has helped the centre bounce back from Covid-era restrictions.

John Grindrod

Greenwich Yacht Club

Location: North Greenwich, London
Designed by: Frankl and Luty
Opened: 2000

The Greenwich Yacht Club is a striking millennium-era landmark providing a unique visual divider between the towering new residences of Greenwich Peninsula and the still remarkably industrial waterfront of Charlton.

Completed in 2000 as a replacement for the club's former premises nearby, the £3.5 million complex was designed by Frankl and Luty with a suitably rugged exposed-steel exterior and comfortingly warm pine interiors. The project includes onshore engineering sheds and an events venue connected by a bridge to a three-storey clubhouse elevated above the River Thames on a repurposed pier.

Offering panoramic views of one of London's most open, dynamic and changing landscapes including the Thames Barrier, Greenwich Millennium Village and Millennium Dome – the clubhouse is open to the public every year for the Open House Festival.

Merlin Fulcher

Commonwealth Games (Etihad) Stadium

Location: Sportcity, Manchester
Designed by: Arup
Opened: 2002

Now home to Manchester City and known as the Etihad, this stadium was designed and built to host the 2002 Commonwealth Games. Athletics and football require differently proportioned space and seating arrangements. Thus, the stadium was designed to be adapted to its legacy use from the start by way of a temporary north stand that would allow vast quantities of earth to be removed, lowering the bowl by 6 metres (20 feet) and turning a 38,000-seater stadium into a 48,000 one. Eight satellite drums of spiralling pedestrian ramps call to mind those at Milan's San Siro. Its overall aesthetic is informed by a novel cable-stay roof that enables column-free spectator views. Twelve steel masts support fans of steel cables that in turn carry the roof structure. In its first football incarnation, the stadium was symmetrical and fluid, its undulating form eminently legible in the flat post-industrial lands of East Manchester.

Richard Brook

Clickimin Leisure Complex

Location: Lerwick, Shetland
Designed: FaulknerBrowns
Opened: 2005

Constructed in three phases from 1985, the Clickimin Leisure Complex provided the central star in a constellation of leisure centres across the Shetland Islands. Commissioned by the Shetland Recreational Trust using revenue from the oil industry, the scale of the construction was extraordinary. The complex still constitutes the largest building footprint on Shetland. Partially sunk into the ground to withstand harsh weather conditions, the design is visually modest but significant for its impact, bringing exceptional sports offerings to local communities.

FaulknerBrowns followed the project by constructing centres in Unst, Yell, Whalsay and Scalloway, as well as North, South and West Mainland. All feature similar designs with low-pitched roofs, porthole motifs, timber fittings and internally exposed roof structures: a consistent brand for leisure on the islands. As the Shetland Recreational Trust declared, 'the result is that nowhere in Shetland are you out of reach of the best sports facilities.'

Alborz Dianat

Ascot Grandstand

Location: Ascot Racecourse, Berkshire
Designed by: HOK Sport; Consulting Engineers, Buro Happold; Contractor, Laing O'Rourke
Opened: 2006

Racing correspondent John Rickman wrote in 1952, 'I dream of the day when there will be a dignified and soaring stand at Ascot stretching for more than half a mile down the course, with excellent viewpoints, escalators, lifts, wide stairways and ample weather protection.' Finally, in 2006, HOK Sport's 370-metre (1,214-foot) long, 30,000 capacity stand – the UK's largest – answered that brief. With Royal approval, this being Crown Estate land, the course had to be realigned by 43 metres (141 feet). The front lawns and lower terraces then needed reprofiling to rectify sightline problems. Some likened the full-length atrium to an airport terminal. Architect Rod Sheard, however, called it an 'environmental lung', introducing natural light and ventilation. A newly created 9,000-capacity parade ring, overseen at the stand's rear, also eased historic circulation issues, while a service road ensures that all 265 boxes, seven restaurants and multiple bars can be discreetly stocked with champagne throughout Royal Ascot.

Simon Inglis

Wembley Stadium

Location: South Way, Wembley, London
Designed by: Foster + Partners with HOK Sport
Opened: 2007

By the mid-1990s, the venerable first iteration of Wembley Stadium was outdated and uncomfortable. Completed to the designs of John Simpson, Maxwell Ayrton and Owen Williams in 1923, it had enjoyed a significant place in sporting history, hosting the 1948 Olympics and 1966 World Cup final. The stadium and its beloved Twin Towers were demolished in 2003 to make way for a cutting-edge replacement, designed by Foster + Partners with stadium specialists HOK Sport (now Populous).

The result is the largest stadium in Britain, fitting 90,000 fans into three steeply raked tiers of seating, which are entirely devoid of columns. The vast Wembley Arch does the heavy lifting both visually and structurally; it is the world's longest single-span roof structure, supporting the majority of the roof's weight, and a work of consciously iconic design, which Foster envisaged 'glistening at night on the skyline, a jewel, a tiara!'

Tom Goodwin

Sunderland Aquatic Centre

Location: Stadium Park, Sunderland, Tyne and Wear
Designed by: Red Box Architects
Opened: 2008

When the Sunderland Aquatic Centre opened, it boasted the largest pool in the north of England. The building was designed by Newcastle-based Red Box Architects for Sunderland City Council, and took the shape of a long, flattened tube perched next to the city's Stadium of Light. Inside, the centre contains a wellness centre and two pools, the largest featuring ten lanes, an adjustable hydraulic floor, and seating stands for 500 spectators.

The structure uses 50-metre (164-foot) curved glulam timber ribs, a system which Red Box had used in previous pool commissions but never at such large a scale as at Sunderland. The building is wrapped in 64,600 sq. feet (6,000 sq. metres) of Kalzip aluminium, chosen for its hardwearing qualities in an environment full of heated pool air. To combat the sustainability concerns of filling and heating an Olympic-sized swimming pool, the centre contains harvesting and filtration systems that allow rainwater to be reused as pool water.

Carlos Finlay

Hackney Marshes Sports Centre

Location: Homerton Road, London
Designed by: Stanton Williams
Opened: 2011

Hackney Marshes Sports Centre serves a site with more than 80 football, rugby and cricket pitches – a record-setting number. The building is low-slung and embedded in its landscape, plugging a gap in a band of mature trees. It has two connected volumes: the lower houses the changing rooms; the taller a café/bar and conference rooms. Much in evidence are the controlled detailing and geometries, and the careful handling of materials that are all typical of Stanton Williams, who have developed an award-winning portfolio of work since the 1980s. Here, robustness and security were key considerations. The lower volume is faced with gabion blocks: they weather well and form a framework for climbing plants. Elsewhere, weathered steel cladding includes shutters, which can be opened to allow views of the pitches; perforations in its surface mean that the building glows at night. Overall, the building reconciles the landscape and the human activity of sport.

Alistair Fair

Lee Valley Velodrome

Location: Queen Elizabeth Olympic Park, Stratford, London
Designed by: Michael Hopkins and Partners
Opened: 2011
Listed: Grade II*

Dubbed 'The Pringle', the sensual hyperbolic paraboloid form of the velodrome holds 6,000 spectators and anchors Stratford's VeloPark, with an outdoor BMX track alongside. Clad in 5,000 sq. metres (54,000 sq. feet) of western red cedar, the 250-metre track of Siberian pine was designed by the specialist Ron Webb and installed by 26 carpenters. Sir Chris Hoy, who was on the judging panel for the building, won his sixth gold medal here.

The design used natural ventilation and lighting, a cable net roof and reduced building materials to improve environmental efficiency and lower the building's embodied carbon. The most sustainable building in the Olympic Park, it received numerous accolades including the 2011 RIBA Stirling Prize shortlist and the AJ100 Building of the Year. It was refurbished and reopened in 2014, with a 1-mile (1.6-kilometre) outdoor cycle circuit and 4-mile (6.5-kilometre) mountain bike trail making it the only place to provide for all cycling sports on one site.

Carlos Finlay

London Aquatics Centre

Location: Queen Elizabeth Olympic Park, Stratford, London
Designed by: Zaha Hadid
Opened: 2012

Even before London had been announced the winner of the 2012 Olympics bid, Zaha Hadid had designed a new aquatics centre for the capital. She called it her 'sea-life creature', with a 3,000-ton, wave-shaped aluminium roof. Upon completion in 2012, the building was framed by lateral 'wings' with seats for 17,500 spectators. Its two 50-metre pools and 25-metre diving pool were the epicentre of the Olympic Games' swimming, diving, and synchronized swimming events.

As part of the £292 million scheme to adapt the Olympic Park for public use, the building was modified into a public pool in 2014, with the removal of its lateral wings, the construction of new glazed walls, and the addition of a café, crèche and dry dive training area. Writing in the *Architects' Journal*, Rory Olcayto vowed that when swimming in the new public pool, 'It has to be backstroke. That roof – that ceiling – is a marvel to behold.'

Carlos Finlay

Antur Stiniog Mountain Biking Centre

Location: Blaenau Ffestiniog, Gwynedd
Designed by: Donald Insall Associates
Opened: 2013

Nestled amongst the mountainous slate tips above Blaenau Ffestiniog, the Antur Stiniog Centre bridges the worlds of nineteenth-century industry and twenty-first-century sustainability. Aiming to bring sustainable renewal to a deprived area long experiencing severe economic decline, the centre is at the heart of a network of recreational and world-competitive mountain biking tracks developed in partnership with Communities First volunteers.

Constructed largely from Llechwedd quarry slate waste, the neat and simple complex offers food, showers, workshop facilities and events space, evoking the historic *cabanau* (shelters) and *gweithdai* (workshops) of the quarry workers. Full height glazing to the café and the roof terrace, immerse the user in the glory of the Eryri National Park landscape (the slate quarries now part of Wales's newest World Heritage Site), be there sunshine or (more often) *mwrllwch*. The use of local and sustainable materials, solar gain and grey water recycling have led to a BREEAM Excellent rating.

Susan Fielding

Emirates Arena and Sir Chris Hoy Velodrome

Location: Dalmarnock, Glasgow
Designed by: 3DReid
Opened: 2012

Since the 1970s, Glasgow's regeneration has combined policy and funding initiatives (such as the Glasgow Eastern Area Renewal programme) with festivals and events that provide a focus for activity and community engagement. The XX Commonwealth Games, staged in Glasgow in 2014, saw investment with a clear eye on 'legacy'. This stadium and velodrome comprized the major piece of new sports infrastructure.

It includes a 10,000 sq. metre (108,000 sq. foot) flexible arena, as well as a 8,500 sq. metre (91,500 sq. foot) velodrome (the only one in Scotland), and a 2,500 sq. metre (27,000 sq. foot) Sports Hall, with space and cost efficiencies gained by carefully planning shared 'support' spaces. All this is set beneath a giant metal-clad grid, which thrusts confidently above the concrete clad volumes below.

A Scottish Government study judged the Games' legacy as largely positive, though local opinions vary. In addition to ongoing community and events use, the Velodrome and Arena hosted the 2023 UCI Cycling World Championships.

Alistair Fair

FURTHER READING

Joshua Abbott, *A Guide to Modernism in Metro-land*, London, Unbound, 2020

Christopher Beanland, *Pool: A dip into outdoor swimming pools: the history, design and people behind them*, London, Batsford, 2020

Steve Beauchampe & Simon Inglis, *Played in Birmingham: Charting the heritage of a city at play*, London, Historic England, 2006

Iain Borden, *Skateboarding and the City: A Complete History*, London, Bloomsbury Visual Arts, 2019

Allan Brodie & Geraint Franklin, *Ramsgate: The town and its seaside heritage*, Liverpool, Liverpool University Press/Historic England, 2020

Richard Brook, *Manchester Modern*, Manchester, The Modernist Society, 2023

Cory Buckner, *Cambridge Modernist: The Architecture of David Wynn Roberts*, Crestwood Hills Press, 2022

Susannah Charlton & Elain Harwood, eds., *100 20th Century Buildings*, London, Batsford, 2024

Alan Clawley, *John Madin (Twentieth Century Architects)*, London, RIBA/C20 Society, 2011

Catherine Croft, *Concrete Architecture*, London, Laurence King Publishing, 2005

Alistair Fair, Lynn Abrams, Kat Breen, Miles Glendinning, Diane Watters and Valerie Wright, *Building Modern Scotland: A Social and Architectural History of the New Towns, 1947–1997*, London, Bloomsbury Academic, 2025

Kathryn Ferry, *Seaside 100: A History of the British Seaside in 100 Objects*, Lewes, Unicorn Press, 2020

Geraint Franklin & Elain Harwood, *Post-Modern Buildings in Britain*. London, Batsford, 2017

Ian Gordon & Simon Inglis, *Great Lengths: The historic indoor swimming pools of Britain*, London, Historic England, 2009

John Grindrod, *Iconicon: A Journey around the Landmark Buildings of Contemporary Britain*, London, Faber & Faber, 2023

Elain Harwood, *Art Deco Britain*, London, Batsford, 2019

Elain Harwood, *Mid-Century Modern*, London, Batsford, 2021

Elain Harwood, *Brutalist Britain*, London, Batsford, 2022

Elain Harwood, *Space, Hope and Brutalism: English Architecture 1945–75*, London, Yale University Press, 2015

Elain Harwood & James O. Davies, *England's Post-War Listed Buildings*, London, Batsford, 2015

Simon Inglis, *Football Grounds of Britain*, London, HarperCollins, 1996

Simon Inglis, *Played in Manchester: The architectural heritage of a city at play*, London, English Heritage, 2004

Simon Inglis, *Engineering Archie: Archibald Leitch – Football Ground Designer*, London, Historic England, 2005

Simon Inglis, *Played in London: Charting the heritage of a city at play*, London, Historic England, 2014

Neil Jackson, *Peter Womersley (Twentieth Century Architects)*, London, Historic England/C20 Society, 2023

Ged O'Brien & Simon Inglis, *Played in Glasgow: Charting the heritage of a city at play*, London, Malavan Media, 2010

Lynn Pearson, *Cricket Pavilions*, Stroud, Amberley Publishing, 2024

Lynn Pearson, *Played in Tyne and Wear: Charting the heritage of people at play*, London, Historic England, 2010

Bruce Peter, *Form Follows Fun: Modernism and Modernity in British Pleasure Architecture 1925–1940*, London, Routledge, 2007

Ray Physick, *Played in Liverpool: Charting the heritage of a city at play*, London, Historic England, 2007

Martin Polley, *The British Olympics: Britain's Olympic Heritage 1612-2012*, London, Historic England, 2011

Kenneth Powell, *Arup Associates (Twentieth Century Architects)*, London, Historic England/C20 Society, 2018

Alan Powers, *Modern: The Modern Movement in Britain*, London, Merrell, 2005

Chris Romer-Lee, *Sea Pools: 66 Saltwater Sanctuaries From Around the World*, London, Batsford, 2023

Otto Saumarez Smith, *Boom Cities: Architect Planners and the Politics of Radical Urban Renewal in 1960s Britain*, Oxford, Oxford University Press, 2019

Janet Smith, *Liquid Assets: The Lidos and Open-Air Swimming Pools of Britain*, London, Malavan Media, 2005

ACKNOWLEDGEMENTS

C20 Society would like to thank all those who have contributed to this book or shared their knowledge during its gestation. Particular thanks go to John East who travelled the country from Aberdeen to Falmouth to take new photographs for the book.

Joshua Abbott Printer, runs the Modernism in Metro-land website and tours; author of *A Guide to Modernism in Metro-land* and *Modernism Beyond Metroland*

David Attwood Deputy editor of C20 magazine from 2012 to 2020

Matthew Bliss PhD student at the University of Warwick

Iain Borden Professor at The Bartlett, University College London. Author of *Skateboarding and the City: a Complete History* (Bloomsbury, 2019)

Richard Brook Professor in Architecture and Director of Research at Lancaster University's School of Architecture

Ellie Brown PhD student at the University of Warwick

Katriona Byrne Conservation officer by profession; course director of postgraduate courses in Conservation at Birmingham City University and Deputy Head of the Birmingham School of Architecture and Design

Susannah Charlton Consultant editor specializing in architectural and garden heritage

Catherine Croft Director of C20 Society

Elizabeth Darling Historian of British architectural modernism and of gender and architecture

Adam Dean Works with Historic England in the Midlands, studying for an MA in Conservation at Birmingham City University and author of a *Conservation Management Plan for the Elephant*

Alborz Dianat Architectural historian at University College Dublin

Robert Dowden Member of C20 Society and C20 Projects Coordinator for Friends of Czech Heritage

Robert Drake Former Honorary Secretary and casework committee member of C20 Society

John East interim local authority management and regeneration professional. Unofficial photographer for C20 Society

Alistair Fair Reader in Architectural History at the University of Edinburgh, author of Peter Moro and Partners, and co-author of Building Modern Scotland, a history of the new towns

Susan Fielding Senior Investigator (Historic Buildings) Roal Commission on the Ancient and Historical Monuments of Wales; Chair of C20 Cymru

William Fawcett RIBA Director of Cambridge Architectural Research Ltd

Kathryn Ferry Author of *20th Century Seaside Architecture* (Batsford, 2025)

Carlos Finlay Architectural historian at Alan Baxter and a volunteer for the Twentieth Century Society

Geraint Franklin Author of the forthcoming *High-Tech Buildings in Britain*, which includes several sports and leisure entries

Merlin Fulcher tours director, Open City

Tom Goodwin PhD student at the University of Warwick, researching British architecture in the 1990s and 2000s

Ian Gordon Former competitive swimmer and author of *Great Lengths – The Historic Indoor Swimming Pools of Britain* (English Heritage, 2009)

Simon Green Independent architectural historian

John Grindrod Author of *Concretopia*, *Outskirts* and *Iconicon*

Ewan Harrison Lecturer in architectural history at the University of Manchester and author of a forthcoming monograph on R. Seifert & Partners

Julian Holder Academic and conservationist who was C20 Society's first paid caseworker

Simon Inglis Author and creator of the *Played in Britain* series

Andrew Jackson C20 Society Trustee

Neil Jackson Former C20 Society Trustee and author of the book *Peter Womersley*

David Lambert Director of the Parks Agency

Paul Lincoln Member of C20 Society and a City of London and Open City Guide

Matthew Lloyd Roberts Architectural historian and PhD candidate at the Ax:son Johnson Centre for the Study of Classical Architecture at Downing College, Cambridge

Christina Malathouni Senior Lecturer (Associate Professor), School of Architecture, University of Liverpool

Christopher R Marsden Architectural history and public art researcher

Joe Mathieson Architectural adviser at the Hampstead Garden Suburb Trust and editor of C20's Building of the Month column

Chris Matthews Conservation officer, designer, and author of A History of Nottingham's Council Houses

Euan McCulloch Former Secretary and Co-ordinator of Docomomo Scotland and an active caseworker with the Architectural Heritage Society of Scotland

Andrew Murray Postdoctoral research fellow at the University of Melbourne

Hugh Pearman Architecture writer and chair of C20 Society

Lynn Pearson Architectural historian, author of Cricket Pavilions

Bruce Peter Professor of Design History at the Glasgow School of Art

Alan Powers Writer, teacher and campaigner

Clare Price Cathedrals and Major Churches Officer for the Church of England, formerly Director of Casework at C20 Society

Chris Romer-Lee Co-founder of Studio Octopi, Future Lidos & Swimmable Cities. Author of *Sea Pools* (Batsford, 2023)

Otto Saumarez Smith Teaches architectural history at the University of Warwick and is Chair of C20 Society Casework Committee

Cela Selley C20 Society Trustee (Events Secretary) and keen amateur golfer

Fiona Sinclair Conservation architect and Past President, Glasgow Institute of Architects

Cath Slessor President of C20 Society and contributing editor to *The Architectural Review*

Jonathan Vining Architect and urban designer, trustee of the Dewi-Prys Thomas Trust, and commissioner of the Royal Commission on the Ancient and Historical Monuments of Wales

Richard Walker Visual artist, lecturer, C20 Society tour guide and author of Faro Modernism: 20th century architecture in the Algarve (Batsford, 2025)

Coco Whittaker Head of casework at C20 Society

PICTURE CREDITS

All reasonable efforts have been taken to ensure that the reproduction of the content in this book is done with the full consent of the copyright owners. If you are aware of unintentional omissions, please contact the publisher directly so that any necessary corrections may be made for future editions.

2 © NorthScape / Alamy; 7 © Heritage Image Partnership Ltd / Alamy; 8 © Simon Phipps; 12–13 © Trinity Mirror / Mirrorpix / Alamy; 14 © John East; 15 © John East; 16 © RIBA Collections; 17 © Meaning March / Shutterstock; 18–19 © Bill Waterson / Alamy; 20 © John East; 21 © John East; 22 © John East; 23 © John East; 24 © Mirrorpix / Getty; 25 © John East; 26 © John East; 27 © John East; 28 © John East; 29 © John East; 30 (top) © Toby G. Driver / RCAHMW; 31 © John East; 33 (top) © John East; 33 (bottom) © Gavin Forster Photography. Courtesy of Fusion Lifestyle; 34 © John East; 35 © Historic England Archive; 36 (left) © John East; 36 (right) © John East; 37 (top) © John East; 37 (bottom) © John East; 38 © Findlay / Alamy; 39 © John East; 40–41 © John East; 42 © John East; 43 © John East; 44 © John East; 45 © John East; 46 © Ryan Mckenzie; 47 © Sally Anderson / Alamy; 48 © John East; 49 (left) © John East; 49 (right) © John East: 50 © John East; 51 © John East; 52 © John East; 53 © John East; 54 © John East; 55 © RIBA Collections; 56 © ZUMA Press, Inc. / Alamy; 59 © UrbanImages / Alamy; 61 (top) © Pollard Thomas Edwards; 61 (bottom) © Simon Burt / Alamy; 62 © C20 Society; 65 © Jubilee Park Woodhall Spa; 66 © John East; 67 © John East; 68 © John East; 69 © Stephen Burrows / Alamy; 70–71 © Arsenal football Club; 72 © John East; 73 (left) © John East; 73 (right) © John East; 74 © John East; 75 © Historic England Archive; 76 © John East; 77 © John East; 78 © Peter Barber; 79 (top) © The Broomhill Pool Trust; 79 (bottom) © The Broomhill Pool Trust; 80 © John East; 81 © John East; 82 © John East; 83 © RIBA Collections; 84 © John East; 85 © Courtesy of HES. Records of Dunn and Findlay, architects, Edinburgh, Scotland; 86–87 © John East; 88 © John East; 89 © Laura Hughes / SCRAN; 90 (left) © John East; 90 (right top) © John East; 90 (right bottom) © John East: 91 © John East; 92 © John East; 93 © John East; 94 © Jonathon Vining; 95 © John East; 96 © RIBA Collections; 97 © John East; 98 © John East; 99 © John East; 101 © Britain from Above; 102 Campbell Gray; 105 © PA Images / Alamy; 106–107 © Mark Waugh / Alamy; 109 (top) © PA Images / Alamy; 109 (bottom) © Hazel Plater / Shutterstock; 110 © A.P.S. (UK) / Alamy; 112 © John East; 113 © John East; 114 © Tom McAtee / Alamy; 115 © John East; 116 © RIBA Collections; 117 © RIBA Collections; 118–119 © John East; 120 © John East; 121 © John East; 122 © John East; 123 © John East; 124 © John East; 125 © John East; 126 © John East; 127 © Historic England Archive; 128 © Howard Kingsnorth; 129 © John East; 130 (top) © PA Images / Alamy; 130 (bottom) © PA Images / Alamy; 131 © PA Images / Alamy; 132 © John East; 133 © Neil Jackson; 134 © RIBA Collections; 135 © John East; 136 © John East; 137 © RIBA Collections; 138 (top) © RIBA Collections; 138 (bottom) © RIBA Collections; 142 © Fraser Band; 143 © AK Bell Library Archive; 144 © RIBA Collections; 145 © John East; 146–147 © PA Images / Alamy; 148 © Sheila Halsall; 149 © Freedom Leisure; 150 © John East; 151 © John East; 152 © John East; 153 © John East ; 154 © John East; 155 © Nick Osborne / Alamy; 156 © John East; 157 © John East; 158 © Bradford Museums Archive; 159 © Jonathan Taylor; 160 © Iain Borden; 161 © John East; 162 © RIBA Collections; 163 © RIBA Collections; 164 (top) © T W Dennis & Sons; 164 (bottom) © John East; 167 © FaulknerBrowns; 170-171 © FaulknerBrowns; 172 (top) © Trevor Sempton; 172 (bottom) © Mark Bukumunhe; 174 © John East; 175 © John East; 176 © John East; 177 © Iain Masterton; 178 © John East; 179 © John East; 180 © John East; 181 © John East; 182 © John East; 183 © Jonathon Vining; 184 © Alistair Hunter; 185 © Ove Arup and Partners; 186 © John East; 187 © John East; 188 © John East; 189 © John East; 190 © Richard Bryant; 191 © John East; 192 © Center Parcs; 193 © John East; 194 © John East; 195 Hopkins Architects; 196 © John East; 197 © John East; 198 © John East; 199 © John East; 200–201 © John East; 202 © John East; 203 © John East; 204 © John East; 205 © John East; 206 © John East; 207 © Tom McAtee / Alamy; 208 © John East; 209 © John East; 210 © John East; 211 © John East; 212 © John East; 213 © John East; 214 © TGSPHOTO / Alamy; 215 © John East; 216 © John East; 218–219 © Benjamin Norton; 220 © david pearson / Alamy; 221© John East; 222 © John East; 223 © John East; 224 © Independent / Alamy; 225 © John East; 226 © Dave Donaldson / Alamy; 227 © Dave Donaldson / Alamy; 228 © John East; 229 © PHOTOBYTE / Alamy; 230 © John East; 231 © Nigel Young / Foster + Partners; 232–233 © Nigel Young / Foster + Partners; 234 © John East; 235 © Chris Rout / Alamy; 236 © Hufton+Crow-VIEW / Alamy; 237 © John East; 238 © John East; 239 © John East; 240–241 © Tom Jenkins (don't put in copyright sign); 242 © John East; 243 © John East; 244 © John East; 245 © John East

INDEX

Page numbers in *italics* refer to illustrations

A

Aalto, Alvar 160
Aberdeen, Bon Accord Baths 88, *88*, *89*
Aberdeenshire, Tarlair Outdoor Pool, Macduff *46*, *47*, 64
Adburgham, Jocelyn 81
Addison, Joseph 77
Adie, Button and Partners 145
Adie, George 145
Advertising Association 44
AFL Architects 108
AJ100 238
All England Lawn Tennis and Croquet Club 16, *16–19*, 103, 111
Allies and Morrison 16
Alwyn Lloyd, T. and Gordon 94
Amisfield House, East Lothian 20
Anfield Stadium, Liverpool *106–7*, 111
Angus, Barrie (Cricket) Pavilion 42, *42*
Antur Stiniog Mountain Biking Centre, Gwynedd 244, *244*
Archibald Leitch & Partners 38
Argyll and Bute, Cardross Golf Clubhouse 95, *95*
Armstrong, John Ramsay 25
Arnold Palmer Putting Course, Whitby 153, *153*
Arsenal FC 103, 104
Arsenal Stadium (former), London 68, *68–71*, 103
Art Deco 9, 29
    Arsenal Stadium (former) 68, 103
    Bon Accord Baths 88
    Mounts Bath Leisure Centre 74
    Murrayfield Ice Rink 85
    Royal Birkdale Golf Clubhouse 66
    Smethwick Baths 53
    Tinside Pool 73
    Walthamstow Stadium 50
Arts and Crafts
    Cricket Pavilion, Upper Field, Uppingham School 21, *21*
    Longniddry Golf Clubhouse 20, *20*
    Ynysangharad Lido *30*, 31, *31*
Arup 224
Ascot Grandstand 110, 228, *228*, *229*
Ashworth family 22
Aston Villa 103
Atherden, Ernest 108
athletics 100
    Commonwealth Games (Etihad) Stadium 224, *224*, *225*
    Geoffrey Hughes Athletics Ground 112, *112*, *113*
    Queen Elizabeth II Stadium, Enfield 92, *92*, *93*
Ayrton, Maxwell 100, 103, 231

B

Baker, Sir Herbert 104
Bank Top Brewery 22
Bank Top Conservation Area 22
Barfield, Julia 209
Barrie, J. M. 42
Barrie (Cricket) Pavilion, Hill of Kirriemuir 42, *42*
Barry, Sir Gerald 128
Bassett-Lowke, W. J. 74
BDP 16
Beaconsfield Golf Clubhouse 14, *14*
the Beatles 53
Beech, Gerald 112
Behrens, Peter 74
Bell's Sports Centre, Perth *142*, 143, *143*
Beney, Paul 116
Benson, Philip 44
Berkshire, Ascot Grandstand 110, 228, *228*, *229*
Billingham Forum 9, 10, *138*, 139
Binnie, William 68, 103
Birmingham University 10
Blackpool Corporation 29
Blackpool Open Air Baths 57
Blackpool Stadium 110
Blee, Michael 205
Bletchley Leisure Centre, Milton Keynes 7, *167*, 169, 220
Blur 50
Bobrowski, Jan 104, 174
Bolton Wanderers 110, *110*
Bon Accord Baths, Aberdeen 9, 88, *88*, *89*
Boot, Sir Jesse 34
Borrow, George 178
Botschi, Pierre 163
Bowen Dann Davies Partnership 178, 182
bowling 11
    Ramsgate Croquet and Bowling Pavilions 35, *35*
    Victoria Bowling Club, Norwich 26, *26*, *27*
BREEAM 244
Brierley, Walter 15
Brierley & Rutherford 15
Brixton Recreation Centre, London 186, *186–9*
Brockwell Park Lido, London 60, *61*
Broomhill Pool, Ipswich 60, 64, 78, *78*, *79*
Broomhill Pool Group 78
Broomhill Pool Trust 64
Brutalism 9, 120

Buckinghamshire
    Beaconsfield Golf Clubhouse 14, *14*
    Wolverton Sports Club *162*, 163, *163*
    Woughton Pavilion *180*, 181, *181*
    Xscape 220, *220*, *221*
Buro Happold 228
Button, Chester 53
Button, Frederick 145

C

C20 Society 64, 213
    Concordia Leisure Centre 156
    Finnish Olympic Sauna 91
    Leisure Centres Campaign 11, 173
    Lord's Media Centre 214
    Oasis Leisure Centre 173
    Tinside Pool 73
    Walker Activity Dome 135
    Wrexham Swimming Pool 149
Cadbury's Chocolate Factory, Bournville 25
Cadw 149
Cairns, James Davidson 20
Cambridge University, Corpus Christi and Sidney Sussex colleges boathouse 96, *96*, *97*
Campbell, Alexander Buchanan 144
Canford Cricket Pavilion and Theatre, Wimborne 140, *140*, *141*
Canford School 140
Cardiff, Llanrumney sports pavilion 94, *94*
Cardiff City FC 94, 104
Cardiff University 94
Cardross Golf Clubhouse 95, *95*
Carr, John 104
Castle Irwell Racecourse 108
Center Parcs, Sherwood Forest 169, 192, *192*, *193*
Central Baths, Coventry 10
Chandler, William 50
Chapman, Herbert 68
Chelsea Football Club 108, *109*
Cheltenham Racecourse 104, *105*
Churchill, Winston 50
Cirencester Open Air Pool 57
Civic Trust Award 136, 140
Civil Service Sports Pavilion (former), Duke's Meadows 145, *145*
Clarke, Geoffrey 140
Cleveland Pools, Bath 57
Clickimin Leisure Complex, Lerwick 226, *227*, *227*
Cliftonville Lido, Margate *58–9*, 64

249

Coe, Seb 92
Collcutt & Hamp 14
Colt, Henry Shapland 14, 20
Commonwealth Games
    Commonwealth Games (Etihad) Stadium 224, *224, 225*
    Edinburgh (1970) 150
    Glasgow (2014) 245
Concordia Leisure Centre, Cramlington 156, *156*
Conway, Plas y Brenin, Capel Curig 178, *178, 179*
Coral Reef Waterworld, Bracknell *164,* 169
Cornwall
    Jubilee Pool, Penzance 60, *61,* 63, 64, 67
    Ships & Castles Leisure Pool, Falmouth 202, *202, 203*
Corpus Christi College boathouse, Cambridge 96, *96, 97*
County Durham, Billingham Forum *138,* 139
Couves, L. J., & Partners 123
Coventry 108, 110
    Coventry Central Baths and the Elephant, Coventry Sports and Leisure Centre 116, *116–19*
Craven Cottage, Fulham 103
cricket 100
    Barrie (Cricket) Pavilion, Hill of Kirriemuir 42, *42*
    Canford Cricket Pavilion and Theatre 140, *140, 141*
    Cricket Pavilion, Upper Field, Uppingham School 21, *21*
    Hackney Marshes Sports Centre 236, *237,* 237
    Jesmond Cricket Ground 122, 123, *123*
    Lord's Cricket Ground 10, 104, 111, *194, 195,* 195
    Lord's Media Centre, London 214, *214, 215*
    the Oval 210
croquet
    All England Lawn Tennis and Croquet Club 16, *16–19*
    Ramsgate Croquet and Bowling Pavilions 35, *35*
Cross, Alfred 32
Crystal Palace National Recreation Centre, London 128, *128–31*
Cubism 67
cycling
    Antur Stiniog Mountain Biking Centre 244, *244*
    Emirates Arena and Sir Chris Hoy Velodrome 245, *245*
    Lee Valley Velodrome 238, *238, 239–41*

D
Dam Park Stadium, Ayr 120, *120, 121*
Darbourne & Darke 109
Davidson, John B. 143
Davyhulme Park Golf Club, Flixton 76, *76*
De la Warr Pavilion, Bexhill-on-Sea 60
Deacon, Basil C. 35
Dean, Christopher 185
Denys Lasdun and Partners, University of Liverpool Sports Centre *8*
Derby 108
Derksen, Piet 192
Design and Industries Association 74

Devey, George 81
Devon, Tinside Pool, Plymouth 72, 73, *73*
Djanogly Gallery, Nottingham 34
Dollan, Patrick 144
Dollan Baths (Dollan Aqua Centre), Brouster Hill 10, 144, *144*
The Dome, Doncaster 173, *198,* 199
Donald Insall Associates 244
Doric style 15, 32, *33*
Dorset, Canford Cricket Pavilion and Theatre, Wimborne 140, *140, 141*
Dower, Michael 168
Doyle, Arthur Conan 42
Drew, Jane 140
Droitwich Spa Pool 60
Dunn, J. B. & Martin 85
Dunn, Richard 159

E
East Kilbride, Dollan Baths (Dollan Aqua Centre), Brouster Hill 144, *144*
East Lothian, Longniddry Golf Clubhouse 20, *20*
East Midlands, Highfields Park, Nottingham 34, *34*
East Sussex
    East Sussex National Golf Clubhouse, Uckfield 204, *205,* 205
    Saltdean Lido 60, 64, 82, *82, 83*
East Yorkshire, University of Hull Sports Centre 132, *132, 133*
Easton and Robertson 57
Edinburgh
    Murrayfield Ice Rink 84, *85,* 85
    Murrayfield Stadium 210, *210, 211*
    Royal Commonwealth Pool 150, *150, 151*
Edinburgh, Duke of 157
Edinburgh Dome, Malvern St James Girls' School 157, *157*
Education Act (1944) 9
Edward VII, King 174
Edwards, Pollard Thomas *61*
Elcock & Sutcliffe 107–8
Elder and Lester 139
the Elephant, Coventry Sports and Leisure Centre 116, *116–19*
Elizabeth II, Queen 50
Emberton, Joseph 44
Emin, Tracey 64
Emirates Arena and Sir Chris Hoy Velodrome, Dalmarnock 245, *245*
Empire Games (1934) 54
The Empire Pool, Wembley 9, 54, *54, 55,* 107
Empire Stadium, Wembley 100, *102,* 103
Enfield Town FC 92
English Gymnastics Society, Swedish Dance Theatre/Gymnasium 80, *81*

English Heritage 63–4, 73
Epsom racecourse 107–8
Epstein, Jacob 68
Essex
    The Rom Skatepark, Hornchurch 160, *160, 161*
    The Royal Corinthian Yacht Club, Burnham-on-Crouch 44, *44, 45*
Etihad Stadium, Manchester 224, *224, 225*

F
Faber, Oscar 104, 157
Faulkner-Brown Hendy Watkinson & Stonor 156
FaulknerBrowns
    Bletchley Leisure Centre 169
    Clickimin Leisure Complex 227
    The Dome, Doncaster 173, 199
    Perth Leisure Centre 196
    Xscape 220
Ferrier, Claude Waterlow 68, 103
Festival of Britain (1951) 9, 128
Finch, George 186
Finchley Lido 63
Finchley Rugby Club 43
Finchley Urban District Council 43
Finnish Olympic Sauna, Kent 90, *91,* 91
Fletcher, Roland 53
football 100, 111
    Anfield Stadium *106–7*
    Arsenal Stadium (former) 68, *68–71,* 103
    Bolton Wanderers 110, *110*
    Chelsea Football Club 108, *109*
    Commonwealth Games (Etihad) Stadium 224, *224, 225*
    Dam Park Stadium 120, *120, 121*
    Gala Fairydean Football Club 10, 120, 124, *124, 125*
    Hackney Marshes Sports Centre 236, *237,* 237
    Hillsborough Stadium 10, 100, 107, 108, 111, *114, 115, 115,* 206, 210
    Ibrox Stadium South Stand 38, 39, *39,* 103, 108
    Kirklees Stadium 206, *206, 207*
    Old Trafford 108, 210
    Queen Elizabeth II Stadium 92, *92, 93*
    St James' Park *109*
    Summers Lane Sports Ground 43, *43,* 104, 107
    Wembley Stadium 104, 108, *230, 231, 231–3*
Football Association 115
Football Licensing Authority (FLA) 104
Football World Cup (1966) 231
Foster + Partners 104, 231
Frankl and Luty 223
Franklin & Deacon 35
Friends of City Baths 32
Friends of Tarlair 47
Fry, Maxwell 140
Fulham Football Club 103

Fusion Leisure 78
Fusion Lifestyle 32
Future Systems 111, 214

G
G-Force 160
Gala Fairydean Football Club 10, 120, 124, *124*, *125*
Geoffrey Hughes Athletics Ground 112, *112*, *113*
Gilbert, Wallis 145
Gillinson Barnett & Partners 154, 165–6, 169, 173
Girton College, Cambridge 96
Glasgow
    Emirates Arena and Sir Chris Hoy Velodrome 245, *245*
    Ibrox Stadium South Stand *38*, 39, *39*, 103, 108
Godwin, Michael 157
Godwin and Cowper 157
golf
    Arnold Palmer Putting Course, Whitby 153, *153*
    Beaconsfield Golf Clubhouse 14, *14*
    Cardross Golf Clubhouse 95, *95*
    Davyhulme Park Golf Club, Flixton 76, *76*
    East Sussex National Golf Clubhouse, Uckfield *204*, 205, *205*
    Longniddry Golf Clubhouse 20, *20*
    Royal Birkdale Golf Clubhouse, Southport 66, *66*
    Shirley Golf Club *98*, 99, *99*
Gooday, Leslie 136
Goodwood racecourse 104
    March Stand, West Sussex 174, *174*, *175*
Gordon, Alex 94
Gosford Estate, East Lothian 20
Gradidge, Roderick 213
grandstands
    Ascot Grandstand 110, 228, *228*, *229*
    Grace Stand, Towcester Racecourse *212*, 213
    Ibrox Stadium South Stand, Glasgow *38*, 39, *39*, 103, 108
    March Stand, Goodwood Racecourse 174, *174*, *175*
    Mound Stand, Lord's, London *194*, 195, *195*
    North Stand, Hillsborough *114*, 115, *115*
    Summers Lane Sports Ground 43, *43*, 104, 107
Grange-over-Sands Lido 64
Greater London
    Queen Elizabeth II Stadium 92, *92*, *93*
    Richmond Baths 136, *136*, *137*
Greater Manchester, Davyhulme Park Golf Club, Flixton 76, *76*
Greenwich Yacht Club *222*, 223, *223*
greyhound racing, Walthamstow Stadium, London 50, *50*, *51*
Grillet, Christophe 96
Grimshaw 16
Grimshaw, Nicholas 111, 185
Gwynedd

Antur Stiniog Mountain Biking Centre 244, *244*
Plas Menai (National Outdoor Centre for Wales), Caernarfon 182, *182*, *183*
gymnasiums, Swedish Dance Theatre/Gymnasium, English Gymnastics Society *80*, 81

H
Hackney Marshes Sports Centre, London 236, 237, *237*
Hadid, Zaha 243
Hamp, Stanley Hinge 14
Harrison, Percival T. 43, 104, 107
Harvey, Robert 152
Harwood, Elain 140
Havers, Albert 26, *26*
Henley Royal Regatta Headquarters *190*, 191, *191*
Hermes, Gertrude 49
Hesketh, Lord Alexander 213
Hickey, Maurice 120
High Tech design 195, 199, 213
Highfields Park, Nottingham 34, *34*
Hillsborough Stadium, Sheffield 10, 100, 107, 108, 111, 206, 210
    North Stand *114*, 115, *115*
Historic Scotland 64
historicpools.co.uk 64
HOK Sport 104, 228, 231
Hollamby, Ted 186
Holmes Miller 210
Hopkins, Michael 111, 195, 238
Hopkins Architects 16
Howard, Peter 181
Howard Lobb Partnership 174
Hoy, Sir Chris 238, 245
Hull University 10
Humperdinck, Engelbert 199
Hunt, Anthony 206
Husband & Co. 107, 115

I
Ibrox Stadium South Stand, Glasgow *38*, 39, *39*, 103, 108
ice rinks
    Murrayfield Ice Rink *84*, 85, *85*
    Oxford Ice Rink *184*, 185, *185*
Italian Renaissance style 35

J
J. B. Dunn & Martin 85
J. C. Prestwich & Sons 74
Jan Bobrowski and Partners 174
Jäntti, Toivo 91
Jarman, Derek 140
Jesmond Cricket Ground *122*, 123, *123*
Jockey Club, Newmarket *52*, 52
John Laing Construction 192

Johnson-Marshall 150
Jones, R. W. H. 60, 82
Jubilee Pool, Penzance 60, *61*, *63*, *64*, 67

K
Keele University 10
Kent
    Finnish Olympic Sauna, Aylesford *90*, 91, *91*
    Ramsgate Croquet and Bowling Pavilions 35, *35*
    Swedish Dance Theatre/Gymnasium, English Gymnastics Society, Nonington *80*, 81
King Edward VI Grammar School sports pavilion, Stratford-upon-Avon 152, *152*
Kings House School, Richmond 145
Kirklees Stadium, Huddersfield 103, 206, *206*, *207*
Kirriemuir Regeneration Group 42

L
Laing O'Rourke 228
Lakeside Arts Centre, Nottingham 34
Lancashire
    Royal Birkdale Golf Clubhouse, Southport 66, *66*
    Stanley Park, Blackpool 28, *29*, *29*
    Tennis Clubhouse, Bank Top 22, *22*, *23*
Lansbury's Lido, Hyde Park *56*, 57
Lasdun, Denys and Partners 8
Latham, Captain Frank 60, *61*, 67
Latymer Upper School, London
    boat house *126*, 127, *127*
    former squash court *48*, 49
Le Corbusier 205
Lee Valley Velodrome, London 238, *238*, *239–41*
leisure and sports centres 164–73
    Bell's Sports Centre *142*, 143, *143*
    Billingham Forum *138*, 139
    Bletchley Leisure Centre 220
    Brixton Recreation Centre 186, *186–9*
    Clickimin Leisure Complex 226, *227*, 227
    Concordia Leisure Centre 156, *156*
    The Dome, Doncaster 173, *198*, 199
    Hackney Marshes Sports Centre 236, 237, *237*
    Llanrumney sports pavilion 94, *94*
    Mounts Bath Leisure Centre 74, *74*, *75*
    Oasis Leisure Centre 154, *154*, *155*, 173
    Perth Leisure Centre 169, *196*, 196, *197*
    Richard Dunn Sports Centre 158, *159*, *159*, *172*, 173
    The Sun Centre *164*, 165, 173
    University of Hull Sports Centre 132, *132*, *133*
    Walker Activity Dome *134*, 135, *135*
    Xscape 220, *220*, *221*
leisure parks, Center Parcs, Sherwood Forest 169, *192*, 192, *193*
Leitch, Archibald 39, 100, 103
Lewis, Granville 116

lidos 9, *56–65*
   Broomhill Pool, Ipswich 60, 64, 78, *78*, *79*
   Jubilee Pool, Penzance 60, *61*, 63, 64, *67*
   Saltdean Lido 60, 64, 82, *82*, *83*
   Tinside Pool, Plymouth 72, *73*, *73*
   Ynysangharad Lido, Pontypridd *30*, 31, *31*, 64
Lightfoot Sports Centre *134*, 135, *135*
Liverpool Architecture and Design Trust Award 209
Liverpool Football Club *106–7*
Liverpool University 10
Liverpool Watersports Centre *208*, 209, *209*
Livingston Development Corporation 177
Livingston Skatepark *176*, *176*
Llanrumney sports pavilion 94, *94*
Lloyd, T. Alwyn 94
Lobb Partnership 103, 104, 110, 206
Lobb Sports Architecture 217
Localism Act (2011) 63
London
   All England Lawn Tennis and Croquet Club 16, *16–19*, 103
   Arsenal Stadium (former) 68, *68–71*, 103
   Brixton Recreation Centre *186*, *186–9*
   Civil Service Sports Pavilion (former), Duke's Meadows 145, *145*
   Crystal Palace National Recreation Centre *128*, *128–31*
   The Empire Pool, Wembley 54, *54*, *55*, 107
   Greenwich Yacht Club *222*, 223, *223*
   Hackney Marshes Sports Centre *236*, 237, *237*
   Latymer Upper School Boat House *126*, 127, *127*
   Latymer Upper School (former) squash court *48*, 49
   Lee Valley Velodrome *238*, *238*, *239–41*
   London Aquatics Centre *242*, 243

   London Fields lido 60
   Lord's Cricket Ground 10, 104, 111, *194*, 195, *195*, 214, *214*, *215*
   Polytechnic Stadium 77, *77*
   Porchester Centre 36, *36*, *37*
   Summers Lane Sports Ground 43, *43*, 104, 107
   Walthamstow Stadium 50, *50*, *51*
   Wembley Stadium *230*, 231, *231–3*
London Aquatics Centre *242*, 243
London County Council 57, 60
London Marathon 77
London Olympic Games
   1948 54, 77, 91, 231
   2012 11, 16, 243
Longniddry Golf Clubhouse 20, *20*
Lord's Cricket Ground, London 10, 104, 111
   Media Centre 214, *214*, *215*
   Mound Stand *194*, 195, *195*
Lowe, William 31

M
Macartney, William 107
McCutcheon, Alfred E. 76
Macgregor, J. E. M. 49
Mackintosh, Charles Rennie 74
McLauchlan, E. 60, 78
McLellan, Michael 116
McRobbie, Alexander 88
Madin, John 99
Maine Road Stadium, Manchester 103
Malvern St James Girls' School, Worcestershire, Edinburgh Dome 157, *157*
Manchester City 103, 224
Manchester United 108
Mandela, Nelson 186
Margaret, Princess 140
Marks, David 209
Marks Barfield Architects 209
Marsh, Julian 34
Martin, Leslie 132
Marylebone Cricket Club 195
Mather & Nutter 108
Matthew, Robert 150
Mawson, Alec 92
Mawson, E. Prentice 60
Mawson, Thomas 29, 60
Meagher, Mary 185
Merseyside
   Geoffrey Hughes Athletics Ground 112, *112*, *113*
   Liverpool Watersports Centre *208*, 209, *209*
Merseyside Development Corporation 209
Michael Blee Whittaker Partnership 205
Michael Hopkins and Partners 195, 238
Middlesbrough 108
Millennium Stadium, Cardiff 104, *216*, 217, *217*
Miller, John 47
Miller Partnership 108, 210
Millwall 108
Milne, A. A. 42
Milton Keynes 110
Milton Keynes Development Corporation (MKDC) 163, 181
Miners' Welfare Fund 31, 64
Mitchison, Dick 49
Mitchison, Naomi 49
Moderne design 53, 82, 95
modernism 9, 10
Moore, Tim 173
Morley Horder, Percy 34
mountain biking
   Antur Stiniog Mountain Biking Centre, Gwynedd *244*, *244*
   Lee Valley Velodrome, London 238
Mounts Bath Leisure Centre, Upper Mounts 74, *74*, *75*

multi-functional leisure centres 9
Murrayfield Ice Rink, Edinburgh *84*, 85, *85*
Murrayfield Stadium, Edinburgh 85, 210, *210*, *211*

N
Narro Associates 124
National Eisteddfod of Wales 182
National Heritage Lottery 11, 29, 64, 78
National Lido of Wales *30*, 31, *31*, 64
National Outdoor Centre, Capel Curig *178*, *178*, *179*
National Outdoor Centre for Wales, Caernarfon 178, 182, *182*, *183*
National Recreation Centre, Crystal Palace 9
Neo-Georgian style *32*, *32*, *33*, 52
Neo-Tudor style 22
Nervi, Pier Luigi 43, 124, 144
Neutra, Richard 150
New Eagley Mills 22
Newcastle Cricket Club 123
Nicholas & Dixon-Spain 32
Nicholas Grimshaw and Partners 185
Nonington College of Physical Education 81
Norfolk, Victoria Bowling Club 26, *26*, *27*
North Yorkshire
   Arnold Palmer Putting Course, Whitby 153, *153*
   York Racecourse clock tower and indicator boards 15, *15*
Northamptonshire
   Mounts Bath Leisure Centre, Upper Mounts 74, *74*, *75*
   Towcester Racecourse, Grace Stand *212*, 213
Northolt Park Racecourse, London 104
Northumberland
   Concordia Leisure Centre, Cramlington 156, *156*
   Jesmond Cricket Ground *122*, 123, *123*
   Northumberland Baths, Newcastle upon Tyne *32*, *32*, *33*
   Walker Activity Dome, Newcastle upon Tyne *134*, 135, *135*
Northumberland County Cricket Club 123
Norwich 110
Noscoe, Robin 140
Nottingham Forest 108
Nottinghamshire, Center Parcs, Sherwood Forest 169, *192*, *192*, *193*

O
Oasis (band) 154
Oasis, Holborn 60
Oasis Leisure Centre, Swindon 11, 154, *154*, *155*, 173
Olcayto, Rory 243
Old Trafford, Manchester 108, 210
Oldenburg, Claes 60
Olympic Games
   London (1948) 54, 77, 91, 231
   London (2012) 11, 16, 243

Omond, Kenny 177
The Open 66
Oscar Faber and Partners 157
outdoor centres
    Plas Menai (National Outdoor Centre for Wales), Caernarfon 178, 182, *182*, *183*
    Plas y Brenin (National Outdoor Centre), Capel Curig 178, *178*, *179*
the Oval 210
Ove Arup & Partners 124, 132, 192
Oxford City Stars 185
Oxford Ice Rink *184*, 185, *185*
Oxford Ice Skating Trust 185
Oxfordshire, Henley Royal Regatta Headquarters *190*, 191, *191*

P
Palmer, Arnold 153
parks
    Highfields Park, Nottingham 34, *34*
    Stanley Park, Blackpool 28, 29, *29*
Parliament Hill lido 60
Peach, Charles Stanley 16, 103
Pells Pool, Lewes 57
Pendennis Leisure 202
Penrhyn, Lord 178
Perth
    Bell's Sports Centre *142*, 143, *143*
    Perth Leisure Centre 169, *170–1*, 196, *196*, *197*
Peterborough Lido 59, 60
Pevsner, Nikolaus 107
Plas Menai (National Outdoor Centre for Wales), Caernarfon 178, 182, *182*, *183*
Plas y Brenin (National Outdoor Centre), Capel Curig 178, *178*, *179*
Pollokshields, Glasgow 11
'Polytechnic' Marathon 77
Polytechnic Stadium, Chiswick, London 77, *77*
Populous 104, 111, 231
Porchester Centre, London 36, *36*, *37*
Portobello Bathing Pool, Edinburgh 107
postmodernism 11
Potiriadis, Mark 169
Potter, A. N. 76
Prestatyn seaside pool 57
Prestwich, J. C. & Sons 74
Principality Stadium, Cardiff *216*, 217, *217*
The Prodigy 199
Purcell Architects 15
Purley Way Lido, Croydon 59
Puutalo Oy 91

Q
Queen Elizabeth II Stadium, Enfield 92, *92*, *93*

Queen Elizabeth Olympic Park, Stratford, London 238–43

R
R Seifert & Partners 127
racecourses 107–8
    Ascot 110–11, 228, *228*, *229*
    Cheltenham 104, *105*
    Epsom 107–8
    Goodwood 104, 174, *174*, *175*
    Jockey Club, Newmarket 52, *52*
    Towcester *212*, 213
    York Racecourse 15, *15*
Radiohead 199
Ramsgate Croquet and Bowling Pavilions 35, *35*
Rangers 103
recreation centres *see* leisure and sports centres
Red Box Architects 234
Reed Paper Group 91
Reeve & Reeve 107–8
Reiach and Hall Architects 124
Rhyl, The Sun Centre *164*, 165, 173
RIBA 26, 94, 104, 112, 154, 182, 206, 209, 238
Richard Dunn Sports Centre, Odsal *158*, 159, *159*, 172, 173
Richards, John 150
Richardson, Albert 52
Richmond Baths, Greater London *136*, *136*, *137*
Richmond Ladies Swimming Club 136
Rickman, John 228
Ridley, Tom 124, 132
RMJM 150
Roberts, David 96
Roberts, Francis 213
Robertson, Andrew & Partners 202
Rogers, Richard 220
roller-skating 9
Rolt, Adrian 160
The Rom Skatepark, Hornchurch 160, *160*, *161*
Rous, Sir Stanley 115
Rowbotham, H. A. 60, *61*
Rowheath Pavilion, Bournville 24, 25, *25*
rowing
    Henley Royal Regatta Headquarters *190*, 191, *191*
    Latymer Upper School Boat House *126*, 127, *127*
Royal Birkdale Golf Clubhouse, Southport 66, *66*
Royal Commonwealth Pool, Edinburgh 150, *150*, *151*
The Royal Corinthian Yacht Club, Burnham-on-Crouch 44, *44*, *45*
Royal Grammar School, Jesmond 123
Royal Horticultural Halls, Westminster 53, 74
rugby 100
    Hackney Marshes Sports Centre *236*, 237, *237*
    Millennium Stadium, Cardiff 104, *216*, 217, *217*
    Murrayfield Stadium, Edinburgh 210, *210*, *211*

Summers Lane Sports Ground 43, *43*, 104, 107
Rugby World Cup (1999) 217
Rutland, Cricket Pavilion, Upper Field, Uppingham School 21, *21*

S
S&P 169
Safety of Sports Grounds Act (1975) 104
St Andrews University 10
St James' Park, Newcastle *109*
Saltdean Lido 60, 64, 82, *82*, *83*
Sargent, Peter 154, 165–6, 168, 169
Sargent and Potiriadis 169
saunas, Finnish Olympic Sauna, Kent 90, 91, *91*
SAVE 73
School of Arts and Crafts, Northampton 74
Scottish Borders, Gala Fairydean Football Club 120, 124, *124*, *125*
Scottish Rugby Union 85, 210
Scottish Sports Council 177
Scunthorpe United 115
SDC 21
Seifert, R & Partners 127
Serpentine, Hyde Park *56*, 57
Shakespeare Memorial Theatre, Stratford-upon-Avon 49
Sharples, Joseph 209
Sheard, Rod 217, 228
Sheeran, Ed 199
Sheffield Wednesday 115
Shepherd, Herbert 36
Shetland, Clickimin Leisure Complex, Lerwick *226*, 227, *227*
Shetland Recreational Trust 227
Ships & Castles Leisure Pool, Falmouth 202, *202*, *203*
Shirley Golf Club 98, *99*, 99
Sidney Sussex College, Cambridge, boathouse 96, *96*, *97*
Silva, Minette de 205
Simpson, Sir John William 100, 103, 231
Skate Park Construction Ltd 160
skateparks 9
    Livingston Skatepark 176, *176*
    The Rom Skatepark, Hornchurch 160, *160*, *161*
Skempton, Trevor 159, 172, 173
Slessor, Cath 199
Smethwick Baths 53, *53*, 74
Smith, Janet 63–4
South Ayrshire, Dam Park Stadium, Ayr 120, *120*, *121*
South Bay Bathing Pool, Scarborough 73
South Yorkshire
    The Dome, Doncaster 173, *198*, 199
    Hillsborough Stadium, North Stand, Sheffield *114*, 115, *115*
Spence, Basil 205
Sport England 178

Sport Wales 182
sports and leisure centres 164–73
  Bell's Sports Centre *142*, 143, *143*
  Billingham Forum *138*, 139
  Bletchley Leisure Centre 220
  Brixton Recreation Centre 186, *186–9*
  Clickimin Leisure Complex 226, 227, *227*
  Concordia Leisure Centre 156, *156*
  Crystal Palace National Recreation Centre 128, *128–31*
  The Dome, Doncaster 173, *198*, 199
  Hackney Marshes Sports Centre 236, 237, *237*
  Llanrumney sports pavilion 94, *94*
  Mounts Bath Leisure Centre 74, *74*, *75*
  Oasis Leisure Centre 154, *154*, *155*, 173
  Perth Leisure Centre 169, *196*, 196, *197*
  Richard Dunn Sports Centre 158, 159, *159*, 172, 173
  The Sun Centre *164*, 165, 173
  University of Hull Sports Centre 132, *132*, *133*
  Walker Activity Dome *134*, 135, *135*
  Xscape 220, *220*, *221*
sports clubs, Wolverton Sports Club 162, 163, *163*
The Sports Council 6
Sports Council for Wales 182
sports grounds, Queen Elizabeth II Stadium, Enfield 92, *92*, *93*
Sports Grounds Safety Authority 104
sports halls and pavilions
  Civil Service Sports Pavilion (former), Duke's Meadows 145, *145*
  Edinburgh Dome, Malvern St James Girls' School 157, *157*
  King Edward VI Grammar School, Stratford-upon-Avon 152, *152*
  Rowheath Pavilion, Bournville 24, 25, *25*
  Woughton Pavilion, Milton Keynes *180*, 181, *181*
squash courts, Latymer School, Hammersmith *48*, 49
stadiums 100–11
  Anfield Stadium, Liverpool *106–7*
  Arsenal Stadium (former), London 68, *68–71*, 103
  Bolton Wanderers 110, *110*
  Chelsea Football Club 108, *109*
  Commonwealth Games (Etihad) Stadium, Manchester 224, *224*, *225*
  Crystal Palace National Recreation Centre, London 128, *128–31*
  Dam Park Stadium, Ayr 120, *120*, *121*
  Hillsborough Stadium, Sheffield 10, 100, 107, 108, 111, 114, 115, *115*, 206, 210
  Ibrox Stadium South Stand *38*, 39, *39*, 103, 108
  Kirklees Stadium, Huddersfield 206, *206*, *207*
  Millennium Stadium, Cardiff 104, *216*, 217, *217*
  Murrayfield Stadium, Edinburgh 210, *210*, *211*
  Old Trafford, Manchester 108
  Polytechnic Stadium, Chiswick, London 77, *77*

Queen Elizabeth II Stadium, Enfield 92, *92*, *93*
St James' Park, Newcastle *109*
Walthamstow Stadium, London 50, *50*, *51*
Wembley Stadium, London 104, 108, *230*, 231, *231–3*
Stamford Bridge, London 108, *109*
stands and grandstands
  Ascot Grandstand 110, 228, *228*, *229*
  Grace Stand, Towcester Racecourse *212*, 213
  Ibrox Stadium South Stand, Glasgow *38*, 39, *39*, 103, 108
  March Stand, Goodwood Racecourse 174, *174*, *175*
  Mound Stand, Lord's, London *194*, 195, *195*
  North Stand, Hillsborough *114*, 115, *115*
  Summers Lane Sports Ground 43, *43*, 104, 107
Stanley Park, Blackpool 28, *29*, 29
Stanton Williams 237
Stirling Prize 214
Stockbroker's Tudor 26, *26*
Stoke 108
Suffolk
  Broomhill Pool, Ipswich 60, 64, 78, *78*, *79*
  Jockey Club, Newmarket 52, *52*
Summers Lane Sports Ground, London 43, *43*, 104, 107
The Sun Centre, Rhyl *164*, 165, 173
Sunderland Aquatic Centre 234, *234*, *235*
Sussex University 10
Swedish Dance Theatre/Gymnasium, English Gymnastics Society *80*, 81
swimming 9, 10, 166
  Billingham Forum *138*, 139
  Bon Accord Baths, Aberdeen 88, *88*, *89*
  Broomhill Pool, Ipswich 60, 64, 78, *78*, *79*
  Concordia Leisure Centre, Cramlington 156, *156*
  Coventry Central Baths and the Elephant, Coventry Sports and Leisure Centre 116, *116–19*
  Crystal Palace National Recreation Centre, London 128, *128–31*
  Dollan Baths (Dollan Aqua Centre), Brouster Hill 144, *144*
  The Empire Pool, Wembley 54, *54*, *55*, 107
  Jubilee Pool, Penzance 60, *61*, 63, 64, *67*
  lidos 56–65
  Liverpool Watersports Centre *208*, 209, *209*
  London Aquatics Centre *242*, 243
  Mounts Bath Leisure Centre, Upper Mounts 74, *74*, *75*
  Northumberland Baths, Newcastle upon Tyne 32, *32*, *33*
  Oasis Leisure Centre, Swindon 154, *154*, *155*, 173
  Porchester Centre 36, *36*, *37*
  Richmond Baths, Greater London 136, *136*, *137*
  Royal Commonwealth Pool, Edinburgh 150, *150*, *151*
  Saltdean Lido 60, 64, 82, *82*, *83*
  Ships & Castles Leisure Pool, Falmouth 202, *202*, *203*
  Smethwick Baths 53, *53*
  Sunderland Aquatic Centre 234, *234*, *235*

Tarlair Outdoor Pool, Macduff 46, 47, 64
Tinside Pool, Plymouth 72, 73, *73*
Wrexham Swimming Pool (Wrexham Waterworld) 148, 149, *149*
Ynysanghard Lido, Pontypridd 30, 31, *31*, 64

T
T. Alwyn Lloyd and Gordon 94
Tapper, Michael 21, *21*
Tapper, Walter John 21
Tarlair Outdoor Pool, Macduff *46*, 47, 64
Taylor, Lord Justice 104, 111
Taylor Report (1990) 100, 108, 110, 206, 210
tennis 11
  All England Lawn Tennis and Croquet Club 16, *16–19*, 103, 111
  Tennis Clubhouse, Bolton 22, *22*, *23*
Terry Farrell Partnership 191
Thirties Society 62, 63
Thomas Mawson & Sons 29
Thomson, Frank Drummond 42
Thorburn & Partners 108
Tinside Action Group 73
Tinside Pool, Plymouth 63, 72, 73, *73*
Tomlins, Freddie 85
Tonge, George E. 66
Tooting Bec Lido 63
Torvill, Jayne 185
Tottenham FC 104, 108
Towcester Racecourse, Grace Stand *212*, 213
Trent, Lord 34
Trent Building, Highfields Park, Nottingham 34
Trentham Park lido 63
Trinity Christian Centre Trust 25
Tudor Grange, Solihull 9
Turkish baths, Porchester Centre 36, *36*
Twentieth Century Society *see* Thirties Society
Twickenham Rugby Stadium 100, *101*, 104, 108, 110
Tyne and Wear, Sunderland Aquatic Centre 234, *234*, *235*

U
UCI Cycling World Championships (2023) 245
universities 9–10
University College of South Wales and Monmouthshire 94
University of Hull Sports Centre 132, *132*, *133*
University of Liverpool
  Geoffrey Hughes Athletics Ground 112, *112*, *113*
  Sports Centre *8*
Uppingham School 21, *21*
Urquhart, Dee 177
Urquhart, Iain 177

V
velodromes

Emirates Arena and Sir Chris Hoy Velodrome 245, *245*
Lee Valley Velodrome 238, *238*, *239–41*
Victoria Bowling Club, Norwich 26, *26*, *27*

W
Wales Empire Pool, Cardiff 10
Walker, Daphne 85
Walker Activity Dome, Newcastle upon Tyne *134*, 135, *135*
Wall, Sir Frederick 43
Walthamstow Stadium, London 50, *50*, *51*
Warner, Pelham 104
watersports centres, Liverpool Watersports Centre *208*, 209, *209*
Webb, Ron 238
Webster, John James 100
Weddle, Stanley 136
Weekes, Joseph 95
Welsh Rugby Union 104
Wembley Stadium, London 43, 54, 91, 104, 108, *230*, 231, *231–3*
Wemyss, Earl of 20
West Lothian, Livingston Skatepark 176, *176*
West Midlands
Coventry Central Baths and the Elephant, Coventry Sports and Leisure Centre 116, *116–19*
King Edward VI Grammar School sports pavilion, Stratford-upon-Avon 152, *152*
Rowheath Pavilion, Bournville 24, 25, *25*
Shirley Golf Club *98*, 99, *99*
Smethwick Baths 53, *53*
West Sussex, March Stand, Goodwood Racecourse 174, *174*, *175*
West Yorkshire
Kirklees Stadium, Huddersfield 206, *206*, *207*
Richard Dunn Sports Centre, Odsal *158*, 159, *159*, *172*, 173
Westbury Court, Gloucestershire 15
Weston, Richard 182
Whitley Bay Leisure Centre 169
Wibberley, J. 73
WilkinsonEyre 111
Williams, Sir Owen 43, 54, 107, 120, 231
Williams-Ellis, Clough 181
Williamson, F. D. (William Partnership) 149
Williamson, Faulkner-Brown and Partners 135
Wilson, Derek 103, 104
Wiltshire, Oasis Leisure Centre, Swindon 154, *154*, *155*, 173
Wimbledon 16, *16–19*, 103, 111
Wingate and Finchley FC 43
Wolfenden Report (1960) 9, 135
Wolfson College, Cambridge 96
Wolverton Sports Club *162*, 163, *163*

Womersley, Peter 10, 120, 124, 132
Woodhall Spa pool 60, *65*
Worcestershire, Edinburgh Dome 157, *157*
World Stadium Team 104
Woughton Pavilion, Milton Keynes *180*, 181, *181*
Wrexham Swimming Pool (Wrexham Waterworld) *148*, 149, *149*
Wright, Frank Lloyd 136
Wright, Gladys 81
Wright, Lance 165, 166
Wyatt, Benjamin 178

X
Xscape, Milton Keynes 220, *220*, *221*

Y
yacht clubs
Greenwich Yacht Club *222*, 223, *223*
The Royal Corinthian Yacht Club, Burnham-on-Crouch 44, *44*, *45*
Ynysangharad Lido, Pontypridd *30*, 31, *31*, 64
York Racecourse clock tower and indicator boards 15, *15*
Youngs, John 26
YRM 206

The community for modernity.

C20 Society is an independent charity and the guardian of Britain's modern design and architectural heritage.

For over 40 years, we've successfully campaigned to save countless landmarks for the nation: from iconic red phone boxes to Art Deco lidos, Brutalist bus stations to pop-art murals, even helping Bankside power station to become the cathedral of art, Tate Modern.

We believe good design enriches lives and contributes towards thriving communities, yet our shared heritage is under threat more than ever before. Each year our casework team tackle thousands of cases and help to secure listed status for remarkable buildings, while our campaigns lead the debate on the built heritage of the future, advancing environmental arguments and championing community solutions.

To find out more and get involved, visit c20society.org.uk

Together, we can protect the best of twentieth and twenty-first century architecture for future generations.